GOP 2.0

HOW THE 2020 ELECTION CAN LEAD TO A
BETTER WAY FORWARD FOR AMERICA'S CONSERVATIVE PARTY

GEOFF DUNCAN
LT. GOVERNOR OF GEORGIA

Forefront
BOOKS

GOP 2.0
How the 2020 Election Can Lead to a Better Way
Forward for America's Conservative Party

Published by Forefront Books.

Cover Design by Bruce Gore, Gore Studio Inc.
Interior Design by Bill Kersey, KerseyGraphics

ISBN: 978-1-63763-013-6
ISBN: 978-1-63763-014-3 (eBook)

To Brooke and my three sons, Parker, Bayler,
and Ryder, for never leaving my side.
I'll never leave yours.

CONTENTS

PART TWO
A BETTER MESSAGE

PART THREE
THE PET PROJECT: POLICY, EMPATHY, TONE

PROLOGUE

★ ★ ★

THE PRESIDENT WENT DOWN TO GEORGIA

THE CROWDS FASCINATED MY SONS. THEY PRESSED THEIR FACES TO the windows of the Suburban as our detail of Georgia state troopers guided us along the crowded road leading to the airport. The thick lines of cars, trucks, and people along the roadside stretched for what seemed like miles. Nearly everyone they saw wore a red "Make America Great Again" cap. People carried flags and signs that left no doubt how they felt about their president.

As a Republican, the big turnout just days ahead of the 2020 election encouraged me.

While the crowds outside mesmerized our three boys, I thought about what I'd say at that night's rally. As Georgia's lieutenant governor, I'd been invited to speak before the president arrived in Rome, Georgia, two nights before Election Day 2020. I was glad my sons Parker, Bayler, and Ryder could see me speak. Having them see the president speak gave me pause, however. While I think any young person should see a president in person if possible, my wife, Brooke, and I cringed thinking of what *this* president might say in front of our boys and what we'd have to explain afterwards.

The boys' excitement grew as we progressed through the rings of security at the airport. First, we cleared the local police and sheriff and then passed a checkpoint run by the Georgia State Patrol. Finally, the dark suits and explosive-sniffing dogs of the U. S. Secret Service surrounded the Suburban. The kids were charged up like I'd rarely seen them. I thought about how excited I'd been as a young pitcher to meet President George H. W. Bush and bond over our love of baseball while I was playing for the Portland Seadogs, the nearest team to his home in Kennebunkport, Maine.

I didn't know someone could be more excited by a president until now. My boys were already excited about seeing Dad speak at a rally and seeing the president. The Secret Service ratcheted up their excitement even further. I'll admit I was almost as energized as they were. I don't care how old you are or how accustomed to government trappings you become, there's still something thrilling about the aura of the presidency.

Darkness fell early and a full moon rose. Brooke and I felt the temperature dropping. We noticed people replacing their red ballcaps with red stocking caps. We sat awkwardly between the two Republican U. S. Senate candidates who were then engaged in a nasty Republican-versus-Republican campaign against each other, and I was happy to be rescued by the stage manager. On his cue, I walked from my seat into the action.

Two enormous American flags flew from cranes flanking the stage. Behind me, the presidential campaign staff had made sure just the right people holding exactly the right signs filled the grandstand. In front of me were 20,000 to 30,000 fully energized Republican voters. Blinding lights and a cold wind hit me. Music played and chants came and went from the crowd, which was clearly unbowed by the weather. Nobody could deny the energy.

I took my place behind the presidential podium. I knew my sons were watching from the crowd so I would deliver my remarks knowing they'd hear every word. They were my accountability partners that night, as they often are. Their presence would make sure I didn't get caught up in the energy of a crowd and say something that was inflammatory, that was only partially true, or that was unkind. If I did any of those things, I'd have to answer to my boys.

It's been so interesting for Brooke and me to watch our kids develop their own opinions about politics. Regardless of opinion (and we have different opinions), the guiding force in our house is "Love your neighbor." The Duncans know that at the State Capitol, Dad always operates by a guiding principle: "Policy over politics." They've learned I believe that whatever your party, good public policy should lift all boats. I'm a policy wonk and frankly, I don't care who comes up with a good idea. The boys understand I simply want the policy to work well for all Georgians.

And so I closed my speech at the rally with those sentiments. I reminded the crowd (and my sons) how Republican principles can benefit everyone. "Every time we lower taxes, it's not just for Republicans," I said to light applause. "Every time we improve education, it's not just for Republicans, it's for everybody."

At that point, I noticed slightly less applause and several boos. I went on. "Every time we grow the economy or add a job, it's not just for Republicans, it's for everybody." I could tell that public policy wasn't firing up the faithful as it had done in the past. Well, I thought, at least I wouldn't be stealing any of the president's thunder that night.

"Our conservative values are so good and so strong they even help the people who don't vote for us." I said that as much for my sons as for anybody, but several more boos drifted from the crowd. The applause got a little quieter. Someone called out to hear from Marjorie Taylor Greene, a controversial candidate who'd infamously supported QAnon conspiracies and was in attendance that night.

I stood on the stage, looking out at people who'd voted for me just two years ago. Why did I feel like a stranger?

★ ★ ★

A vocal portion of the Republican Party had become unquestioning followers of the man in the White House. He had convinced these good people that if you didn't carry his same tone and support his every decision, you were with *them*, not him. When the president strayed from long-standing Republican positions, his fans went right along, egged on by other party leaders. At the extreme, some acted as if anyone who dissented didn't count—as a member of the party or, increasingly, simply as a citizen. A chilling tone had descended on the party: *You're either with us or against us.*

That's not how you govern a state like Georgia.

I'd been largely able to avoid the GOP's national sideshows because Georgians have always cared more about above-the-ground issues that affect them and their families. So I had been able to focus on issues that really matter to my nearly 11 million constituents here in Georgia: jobs, education, and healthcare.

I had proudly worked across the aisle on big issues such as passing rural healthcare reform with unanimous support and passing hate crimes legislation with only a handful of dissenters.

You can't make policy without the middle. Nor can you lead a state or country—or win big elections—without an inclusive coalition. Bipartisan support is not a sign of weakness. It's something I know Georgia's voters have appreciated and benefitted from in the form of great policy outcomes and less rancor.

But the national party's rightward drift, its increasingly hard lines, and the president's tendencies had concerned me long before this one night.

At the podium, I shifted gears to get the crowd back: "Let's shock the world and send this blue wave back to the beach where it belongs!" That got them. They roared, and I felt them. I understood why the president relishes a good rally. A sea of Make America Great Again hats and waving flags can make a person forget anyone else might hold a different view. I left the stage to deafening chants of "Four more years! Four more years!"

The president arrived behind schedule that night, but the delay didn't dull the crowd's reaction when the lights of Air Force One began descending toward the runway. The faithful erupted anew when America's flagship aircraft taxied to a stop just behind the stage. Wearing a red hat, red tie, and long blue coat, the president of the United States walked down the stairs. "God Bless the USA" played over the speakers. He took the stage to a volume of cheering usually reserved for rock concerts. A "USA" chant began spontaneously followed shortly thereafter by a new chant: "We love you!"

Our 45th president spent his first four minutes on stage rattling off his administration's accomplishments. Then he pivoted and began attacking the media, Democrats, and his other enemies. He spoke for 45 minutes. To me, his rants and cutdowns drowned out his accomplishments, which were many. I wondered what my boys were thinking and what I'd need to unpack for them later. His tone and lists of grievances obscured his policy track record, as they did in almost every other speech. If he'd asked me (which he didn't), I'd have told him to spend 45 minutes talking about his wins.

But the president just couldn't help himself.

★ ★ ★

A year earlier, I'd been finishing my dessert at a luncheon where the president was speaking. A Secret Service agent tapped me on the shoulder. "Lt. Governor Duncan, can you come with me?"

You always say "Yes" to the men with earpieces.

In a side room, the agent said, "The president asked if you could ride in the car with him after the event."

You also say "Yes" to that invitation. The agent whisked me to the waiting motorcade where I stepped inside the heavily armored presidential limousine known as the Beast. A few seconds later, the president of the United States slid into the back seat.

"Did you watch that CNN interview before I left Washington," he immediately asked me. "Did you see that interview?" It was half a day after the interview, and he was still angry about it. "They're intentionally sabotaging me! They used a crinkle lens setting that makes me look old and weak."

"Yes, sir," I said as the motorcade turned onto the street. "We watched it at the Air Force base before you arrived." I'd never heard of a crinkle lens so I dodged the particulars.

He turned to me and asked, "What should I do, Geoff?"

"Mr. President, if you're asking my opinion, I wouldn't say anything. That only lets them know it bothers you and they'll keep doing it. When I was playing baseball, everyone said I didn't throw hard enough. But I didn't address the criticism and I didn't let it bother me. I just kept striking out batters and winning. Mr. President, don't let it bother you, just keep on winning."

"That's really good advice," he said. "Thank you."

Maybe now he'd talk to the waiting press about how his policies were helping Georgia.

Then after pausing for a moment, he added, "But I'm going to say something."

My heart sank a little bit.

Sure enough, when we arrived at our destination, the president of the United States stepped out of the Beast cocked and ready to let loose on CNN instead of talking about how his policies were helping real people.

Although he seemed unable to stop himself from wasting time attacking enemies, that didn't keep him from moments of real success. During the previous four years, the stock market had reached 30,000; three COVID-19 vaccines were developed; the Supreme Court added three conservative justices and the federal bench added 220 more; the tax code received an overhaul; criminal justice reform passed; ISIS collapsed; four Arab countries had recognized Israel; and a new North American trade deal had gone into effect. I remain convinced that if he had pushed that message as relentlessly as he pushed attacks on the media and Democrats, while showing real presidential leadership on the pandemic, he'd have won the 2020 election.

Looking back, perhaps his flaws and consequent loss were our saving grace. We discovered that all the policy wins in the world couldn't compensate for other shortcomings.

★ ★ ★

A moonlit Georgia rolled quietly past the windows as we traveled home from Rome. The hum of the tires eased Ryder and Bayler off to sleep. Everyone else was quiet. I looked outside and thought to myself, *I just addressed a presidential campaign rally in rural Georgia two nights before the election. Does anyone else realize what this means?*

That the president needed to visit Georgia so late in the campaign was alarming. He'd won our historically Republican state by six points in 2016. Four years later, polls showed him tied or behind Democrat Joe Biden.

Changing demographics and four years of his own rhetoric had shifted the electoral equation.

This was a big clue he was in trouble. The president wasn't campaigning in population centers like Atlanta or the suburbs he'd won in 2016; he was going to a county with fewer than 100,000 residents to speak with people who were already voting for him. His campaign was trying to fill a bucket by wringing the last drops of water out of a rag. It's much easier just to pour in more water.

Campaign advisors knew their candidate was so toxic and bent on turning out his base that they couldn't send him anywhere near a major city. He had become increasingly incapable of adding vital independents and suburban voters to the Republican coalition. In fact, he and those echoing him were actively chasing them away.

Some quietly wondered if his preemptive claims that Democrats had rigged the 2020 election would depress his own turnout; if people didn't think their vote mattered, would they show up? But these wild claims stoked his unquestioning fans and so he kept making them. He wanted to feel his base's devotion and anger toward nonbelievers. He didn't have interest in cajoling skeptics or those in the middle. In fact, he vilified them. Even my conservative remarks made me the outsider because I showed consideration for the other team.

It was November 1, 2020, and the GOP had a problem.

That night, I didn't imagine how dire that problem would soon become for my family, our party, and America itself.

Within the month, we found ourselves facing a crisis of confidence in our elections and in our elected officials. The crisis would soon reach the U. S. Capitol and threaten American democracy itself. The president had whipped up a political hurricane of frightening magnitude and its eye settled over Georgia immediately after the 2020 election. Our sixteen electoral votes hung by the slimmest of margins and the nation followed our story intently. It fascinated voters that a conservative state like Georgia might flip.

It terrified Republicans and it infuriated the president, who loudly charged Georgia with rampant election fraud.

We never, *ever* asked for our state to find the national spotlight; we never wanted to experience a storm as violent as this one. But this crisis found Georgia, and it gave me a hard choice to make as lieutenant governor: Did I stay silent and cower as a howling tempest of conspiracy ravaged everything in which I believed? Or did I stand up for truth and for my state?

Deep down, I didn't ever doubt what I would do. I just knew it'd be hard. I don't teach my boys to do the easy thing, however. Here, Dad had to walk the talk.

Not one fiber in my being could line up behind the fraud-and-conspiracy storyline that quickly became the Republican Party's response to losing a national election. As I realized what needed doing, I noticed a familiar nervousness: that feeling I'd get on the mound when runners were on base and a real slugger stood over the plate. I was a pro reliever and so when I got called into a game, our team was usually in a jam. I knew that unsettled feeling.

I also knew how to throw the right pitch.

I chose to stand up for my state and speak up on behalf of the Republican Party I know as America's party. I decided to give voice to reason and what I sure hoped was a silenced majority of conservatives who saw the same facts I did. I hoped to reassure moderates and independents, as well as alienated conservatives, wondering where to turn. Maybe I could inject some light into this temporary darkness. Maybe I could offer hope and grounding for our party, state, and country.

And maybe speaking out would end my political career in a hot minute.

But that would be okay. I'd never planned on being in politics in the first place and some things matter much, much more to me than any election or office.

Granted, I probably wasn't the best messenger. Heck, I got drafted and chose to play pro ball before I even graduated from Georgia Tech. Others certainly had more diplomas, higher offices, and bigger followings than I did.

But the storm landed smack on top of me, and nobody else seemed to be coming to help. I wasn't sure who'd hear my voice above the thunder. Still, someone had to stand up for Georgia and the truth. Someone had to fight for the soul of our Grand Old Party because America desperately needs it to be grand once again. Someone needed to set an honest example for my sons.

So I stepped into the storm. And I got drenched.

INTRODUCTION

★ ★ ★

GOP 2.0

By Election Day—November 3, 2020—I'd lost a lot of faith in the Republican Party leaders and their direction. What faith I still had disappeared during the next ten weeks. In many ways alone, I went through a political washing machine powered by misinformation on a shocking scale. Some days, Brooke and the boys seemed like my only allies. The president and his lieutenants piled on as I simply stated the truth.

Unfortunately, in their words and tone, I could see the future of *their* GOP.

It looked bleak.

There had to be a better way forward for our party after we'd lost the Big Three—the U.S. House, Senate, and White House—and after we'd chased off so many good people who just couldn't stomach the three-ring circus that had become the presidency. Even as I took my lumps from fellow Republicans for debunking election fraud allegations and conspiracy theories, I began imagining a different path for the party of Lincoln, Eisenhower, and Reagan.

With due respect to those titans, I wasn't thinking of a path backward to bygone eras. I was thinking of channeling their spirits along a new path forward—the next iteration of America's great conservative party. One with Lincoln's honesty and graciousness, Eisenhower's smile and wise leadership, and Reagan's optimistic belief in conservatism and America.

I began imagining a party that could win back the country's trust and reclaim majorities in Washington and across the land while protecting those conservative principles a majority of Americans value.

I began talking about GOP 2.0.

GOP 2.0 is not a new party. Instead, it's a better direction for today's Republican Party. Hey, I'm a lifelong Republican and conservative—nobody is chasing me out of my own party.

I see GOP 2.0 as an independent movement that will help us blaze a way forward that can give the Grand Old Party a fighting chance to win back the White House in 2024. If we can pivot quickly enough, we may even be able to win back the U.S. House in 2022 by lifting reasoned Republican candidates in races at all levels, all across the country.

With each passing day, I'm more confident we can do this. I have faith that a building groundswell believes our party *must* make a change.

I know I'm not the only conservative in America who wakes up bone-weary and wishing the past months were just a bad dream.

I'm not the lone Republican who feels in my gut that our party is following the wrong path.

And I'm not alone in believing we can chart a better course.

We dreamers understand the heavy roadblocks party leaders loyal to the former president and his political machine have placed across every path except his, but we are optimists. Our new movement itself is one of optimism. We believe in the power of our ideas.

Good people in the GOP 2.0 movement hope to find positive ways to reorient and maintain the coalition the former president built, while inviting new people to join it. We aim to welcome, not exclude. Encourage, not disparage.

We'll respect people and speak with reason and honesty, even when the truth isn't the easiest answer to hear.

We'll be the adults in the room because today, nobody else is. If we're going to improve our party and our nation, we need straight talk.

★ ★ ★

I had been one of the last baseball players drafted the year I showed up for spring training with the Florida Marlins organization. I was the underdog of underdogs. When we showed up, John Boles, the director of the Marlins' minor league system, told everyone, "Come talk with me one-on-one for ten minutes and I'll tell you honestly where you stand in this organization."

Being a fresh-eyed rookie, I expected he'd use the session to build up our confidence or welcome us to the pros. Well, after our ten-minute visit, I wanted to throw up.

As the last draft pick in camp, I knew I'd have to work extra hard, but I thought I had pitched well enough to make a roster somewhere.

"Geoff," Boles said, "you're decent but to make a roster, you'll need three people to get hurt, three people to get traded, and you'll need to pitch three of your best games ever."

Because of the hard reality John presented me, I pitched my heart out for more than three games. Then, sure enough, three guys got hurt and three guys got traded. His straight talk let me know what needed doing and I made the roster for the Kane County Cougars.

He wasn't honest with me because I was special. There are probably 250 guys around the country who'd have the same story about "Bolesey." He was being honest because he respected me. He wanted me to understand the reality and have the opportunity to succeed.

John Boles taught me as much about myself and about leadership as anyone ever has—and I still keep in touch with him. He showed me first-hand what you can accomplish when someone is honest with you, and my boys have certainly bene-fited from his example. Even though the medicine can be hard to swallow sometimes, you're better off down the road for taking it. You can see your blind spots and your opportunities. You know what really needs doing.

Right now, party leaders are peddling misinformation and telling people what they think people want to hear. Nobody is hearing the truth and both the party and country are careening down a bad path. Party leaders and the people need to hear the truth. Deep down, they know it. Only if we start being honest, respecting one another, and leveling with voters, can the GOP improve, expand our tent, and stop winning or losing by inches and instead win by miles.

Maybe that's easier said than done.

I can tell you, however, that misinformation and manip-ulation have deeply damaged the party. They continue to do so. The GOP is broken. And when the GOP is broken, so is America.

I believe it's time for GOP 2.0 to shine its light through our party's cracks before it's too late. *We* can be the change the party needs right now.

I do realize my hopes may not play out this year, next year, or even in 2024—I'm an optimist, but not naïve. I'm also a perpetual underdog willing to play the long game. And my long game is forging a better future for the GOP.

My secret weapon? The silenced majority: growing legions of conservatives and moderates alike who yearn for a party that can reclaim lost ground and leave behind the politics of dishonesty, disorder, and division. Millions of people are tired—*dog tired*—of leaders who make them embarrassed to be a Republican and who too often force them to defend the undefendable.

Brooke and I have been there ourselves.

Ranks of good Americans have left the GOP or leaned Republican until the party lurched right. Too many reasonable conservatives and moderates can't find a place in today's Republican Party. Many of these individuals feel as if someone pulled their party out from under them.

You may be one of them.

Sometimes, independently thinking citizens like us are shunned for not agreeing with the president on every issue or decision. Sometimes we're ignored and still other times, we're charged with outright disloyalty.

Many of the people in this boat are not partisans, so they don't yell. They talk softly and with reason, so loudmouths often drown them out. They don't seek attention. They usually don't attend party meetings. They don't tell pollsters they're Republicans, so polls based on party affiliation don't reflect their opinions. They don't use Twitter as a political platform.

They may not talk politics or even like politics, but they understand their civic duty. They worry about the direction of America and its conservative party. They want to do something but often feel powerless.

If this sounds like you, let me say this: As lost or uncomfortable as you may feel in the former president's GOP, you are a Republican and your still voice matters—and it can matter even more. Come find your voice in GOP 2.0.

We need a movement that will encourage the party to respect differing views while coming together to rediscover and advance our common view of freedom: that government should empower citizens, not the other way around.

We need to become a party that has solutions that work for a majority of Americans.

We need policies, coalitions, and messages that can win elections fair and square.

We need to think about the legacy we're leaving our children.

★ ★ ★

Those joining the GOP 2.0 movement may appreciate this guideline laid down by Ronald Reagan: Somebody who agrees with me 80 percent of the time is a friend and ally, not a 20 percent traitor.

To add bipartisan diversity—and because I think this is an apropos quote—I'll also share what former New York City Mayor Ed Koch said about policy: "Agree with me on 9 of 12 issues, vote for me. Agree with me on 12 of 12 issues, see a psychiatrist."

No majority party has held power with its members united on every single issue. That wouldn't have been healthy in Koch or Reagan's day and it's certainly not healthy now. When we build a coalition to win back our majorities, we'll have smart, principled Republicans who disagree with one another. When we disagree, let's have an intellectually honest conversation about the real issues, not a shouting match about the politics. Then let's come together and win.

Let's agree to put policy *over* politics.

Maybe we'll learn something.

Maybe we'll win more elections.

If our objective is, in fact, to win big elections and implement conservative policies, Republicans cannot afford to alienate people who agree with us on 9 of 12 issues. Today it seems we alienate people who agree with us on 11 of 12!

We saw firsthand in Georgia where this mentality gets us. We learned what happens when the GOP places a person above party and policy: Democrats turn red states blue.

I hear Republicans fret about what "the other side" might do if unchecked. Well, the one sure way to find out what the other side will do is for the GOP to keep using the same tone and keep losing big elections!

Minority status is where we're headed right now, but we can change course.

★ ★ ★

Here's an idea. Let's focus on refreshing and recharging the GOP and engaging more voters through conservative **P**olicy, genuine **E**mpathy, and a respectful **T**one.

Let's call this our **PET** Project:

- **Policy:** Support smart conservative legislation that can create consensus and help real people solve real problems.
- **Empathy:** Genuinely seek to understand others inside and outside the GOP, and in the process, build a winning coalition.
- **Tone:** Lead by example as we share our ideas and perspectives with honesty, respect, and civility.

My aim for the PET Project is not to convince 50.1 percent of America's voters that Republicans should lead. I want to set a higher bar. Our policies and behavior should convince 60-plus percent of Americans we're leading the country on a prosperous path. You don't get a job to earn just one more dollar than you need to meet the family budget, right?

Friends, I promise that if we work on these three points, we can win big elections and get this entire country moving in the right direction again. Imagine how putting policy over politics, being honest, being thoughtful, and being the adults in the room would improve our approach, grow our influence, and increase our positive impact on real lives.

Instead of putting one person first, we're going to put *Americans* first. We are going to understand people better, engage them, and help them thrive. We are going to be happy warriors for the conservative cause.

If we follow this new heading, Republicans will never again suffer embarrassment like we did in the 2020 election and its aftermath.

I hope you'll read on and let me share how I came to these conclusions and why I believe so strongly that GOP

2.0 represents the best hope for my family and yours, and for conservative ideas, the Republican Party, and America itself.

PART ONE

ELECTION 2020: A SIX-MONTH NIGHTMARE

I woke up the morning after the 2020 election—Wednesday, November 4, 2020—and didn't realize the abrupt turn my life would take before the month ended. Events soon thrust me into a bizarre Twilight Zone as my party created an alternative reality and then turned viciously against me as the GOP cashiered those time-honored principles for which conservatives have always stood.

Six months of election fallout badly damaged the Republican brand and gave me a hard-earned perspective on what the party must do next in order to survive.

1

★ ★ ★

NOVEMBER 2020: THE FRAUD HOAX

WHEN MY FATHER'S JOB FIRST BROUGHT MY FAMILY TO GEORGIA, it was conservative country, led by conservative Southern Democrats. We moved away and came back, and it was still a conservative state. Democrats held majorities at the state capitol but at least in the South, their party hadn't yet shifted left. After three years at Georgia Tech, I traveled the country playing pro baseball for six seasons. When my wife and I came home to Georgia, it was turning red as conservative allegiances changed to the GOP.

We were starting a family so we moved close to our parents in the suburbs north of Atlanta. And today, we still live nearby in suburban Forsyth County, which I represented in the Georgia House of Representatives for five years. Forsyth voters went Republican 71 percent to 24 percent in the 2016 presidential election. The reddest precinct voted Republican 84 percent to 13 percent. Forsyth was GOP country. Suburban counties such as mine sent a political outsider to the White House in 2016.

By 2020, however, these Republican suburban counties had seen a change. In conversations at our boys' schools, the local grocery store, church, and other places, I sensed frustration with the president and dissatisfaction with the Republican Party. Some felt outright alienated. Even in conservative Forsyth County, a disturbing number of people would tell me they liked many of the president's policies but sure wished he'd put down his phone. Many folks agreed his tone and tactics weren't healthy for the party or the country.

The county's demographics were also changing, along with those in many other counties and states. My boys' elementary school changed from majority white to majority Indian. The Asian population nearly tripled from 2010 to 2020 and Black and Hispanic representation also grew significantly. I experienced this change and learned new perspectives.

These changes and the conversations I had with neighbors would prove indicative. In the 2020 election, conservative stalwart Forsyth County saw a 14-point shift *away* from the president. Another suburban Atlanta county, Henry, notched the country's largest swing from 2016 to 2020: 16 points to Biden. The county experienced a 28-point shift toward blue since 2008. Nearby Rockdale notched the nation's second-largest 2020 swing as Biden gained 15 points over Hillary Clinton's 2016 showing.

If the GOP wants to see the future, it can simply look at Georgia.

Our changing population and voting patterns give warning signs, but they can also offer road signs to a stronger party.

Two nights after the November 1 campaign rally in Rome, I brought Brooke and our three boys to an election night party for one of the two feuding Republican U.S.

Senate candidates whom I'd sat awkwardly between before my rally speech. I addressed a happy audience. The candidate seemed on the way to securing a runoff spot, which was fine with everyone there, because we all knew none of the twenty candidates in the special election would capture 50 percent and win outright.

The president also seemed headed for victory. Early returns in Georgia had him leading Joe Biden by more than 8 points and 250,000 votes.

In my role as president of the Georgia Senate, I'd worked hard to reelect 35 Republican senators in 2020. I'd raised money, given speeches, made commercials, shared advice. That night, I saw 34 of 35 senators running strong and likely to win. That success meant all the world to me. I was proud of our candidates and grateful voters seemed to be validating Georgia GOP priorities.

That so many of our state senators were outperforming expectations gave me hope the president would too.

My kids were understandably ready to leave after I spoke— they had school the next day. We packed them into the car and drove home. My family went to bed, leaving Dad to watch returns until midnight. I fell asleep that night pleased our state senate candidates had performed so well and still reasonably optimistic that the president might beat the pollsters again, although I knew final results might take days.

Overnight, as we all know now, Joe Biden closed the gap. The president's lead had shrunk to 3 percent and 118,000 votes by the time I woke up. It would be close for certain.

Along with the rest of the country, I dug in to wait for thousands of absentee ballots to be counted.

Several facts provide interesting context to the wait.

First, the president had for months been suggesting any votes counted after the night of November 3 might be fraudulent or that a lengthy counting process would invite mischief. But laws passed by the Republican legislatures of Georgia and other states prevented absentee ballot counting from beginning prior to election day. So given the unprecedented volume of ballots being received by mail due to COVID-19 concerns, any election official in Georgia could have told you counting would take days.

Republicans upset about counting ballots after November 3 were essentially complaining about their own doing: The laws had been passed by a Republican legislature and signed by a Republican governor.

Second, the president had created another problem that he used to stir doubt about election results. For months, he had pushed the baseless claim that voting by mail invited fraud, even as he voted by mail himself. He effectively politicized the very act of mail-in or absentee voting.

Prior to the pandemic, Colorado, Hawaii, Oregon, Washington, Oregon, and Utah held elections entirely by mail and voters needed no excuse to cast absentee ballots in twenty-nine other states including Republican-run Georgia. The 2016 election saw 25 percent of votes nationwide cast by mailed ballots. Thus, a great body of evidence was available for the 2020 Stanford University study that found voting by mail had no impact on partisan turnout or vote share.

Nor did any evidence support the president's charges that voting by mail led to fraud.

The conservative Heritage Foundation keeps an online database of voter fraud cases, which proved helpful. In the past twenty years, their data shows 143 fraud convictions related to the 250 million ballots cast by mail since 2000. That's seven or eight cases of mailed ballot fraud per year. Nationwide.

If you like numbers like I do, that's a 0.00006 percent fraud rate. Looking at *all* votes cast by mail *and* in person over those twenty years, authorities found just 1,200 instances of fraud.

The president ignored the data and the pandemic. He charged, without basis, that voting by mail invited widespread election fraud. As a result, many Georgia Republicans chose not to vote by mail, preferring to show up in person on November 3. That meant initial election-night results reflected those Republican-leaning ballots from polling locations. As election workers counted mail-in ballots, Joe Biden's numbers began to rise, since those mail-in ballots skewed Democratic. This wasn't evidence of fraud, just evidence of 2020 voting behavior.

It was a problem of the GOP's own making.

By Friday, November 6, Joe Biden had pulled ahead in Georgia's tally. Thankfully, the 34 GOP state senators who were ahead on election night kept their leads and won. At the presidential level, however, it looked like Georgia had flipped. The conservative Republican secretary of state certified the results on November 13—Biden bested the GOP's nominee by 13,558 votes.

The fears I had at the president's rally in rural Georgia were realized, and the uneasy inkling I got from my neighbors in Forsyth County proved warranted. *The president lost an election he might have won had he employed better tone and discipline.*

Prior to November 3, many major polls had projected a Biden victory in Georgia and my gut was telling me the president might lose. I'd also seen worrisome trends in internal polling from our state-senate campaigns. Our senators gained ground during the final weeks, but the same polls showed the president slipping. Still, since so many senators in tight races outperformed, I'd hoped the president might too.

He didn't.

It was clear that a lot of Georgians had voted for a down-ballot Republican state senate candidate but not for the party's headliner.

I had worried his tone would cost him. It did.

Still, when the ballots were counted, part of me wondered how the president lost. Perhaps the results were inaccurate; perhaps mischief *had* occurred, as the president had been predicting for months. After all, the last time Georgia voted for a Democratic presidential candidate was 1992. In 2020, Republicans held all eight statewide offices, including mine.

Despite months of polling showing he might lose the president's actual loss shocked many believers.

Working with our Democratic colleagues, we'd taken steps to protect and improve our elections during the past years. Georgia selected new voting machines that produced a paper trail. The state outlawed ballot harvesting. The secretary of state implemented a signature requirement for absentee-ballot applications, and the Georgia Bureau of Investigation had provided training to help improve the signature-matching process.

Those improvements seemed to allay most Republicans' concerns—at least until the president began assailing, without basis, the security of absentee voting.

The state of Georgia was well-prepared for the 2020 election and did a commendable job handling the curveball thrown by the pandemic. We had record turnout.

The voting process ran smoothly on Election Day, albeit not perfectly. It's doubtful that any statewide election has *ever* gone without some flaw or issue. We always aim to learn, improve, and do even better next time. In 2020, 1.3 million mail-in ballots (primarily used due to the pandemic) nearly overwhelmed our election workers and took days to count, but our teams performed admirably. Importantly, of those 1.3 million absentee ballots, not a single one was challenged prior to Election Day.

As early returns placed the GOP ticket comfortably ahead on election night, Republicans across the state celebrated the results. I understand the White House likewise celebrated. That evening, it seemed that perhaps the election wasn't as rigged as the president had thought.

The coming days saw the lead shift from the Republican ticket to the Democratic one in Michigan and Wisconsin, and then in Pennsylvania and Georgia. The president, who'd been calling the election "rigged" for months (and really since 2016), raised his decibels and unleashed new charges of fraud, all without evidence.

Joining his chorus were a number of his allies and elected officials, none of whom had any more evidence than the president. They levied broad attacks. Even though many had never spent time in our state outside of layovers at the Atlanta airport, they singled us out and became experts on Georgia's shortcomings.

With all the volume and vitriol they could muster, these Republicans lit into our state's Republican leaders, good-hearted election workers, and dedicated volunteers. They even pressured our two U. S. senators to call for the secretary of state's resignation.

Over what? Pure speculation? Over what our officials deemed the most secure election in Georgia history?

It's worth noting none of these detractors had executive responsibility for governing Georgia or Georgia's elections. They just threw mud and stirred up trouble Georgians certainly didn't need or deserve. They all should have known better.

Now, did Georgia have problems during the 2020 election? Yes. Any state with new voting machines, 5 million voters, and thousands of temporary poll workers will experience some problems. Despite the challenges related to equipment and volume, however, all indicators pointed to a well-run election. Any issues uncovered or experienced proved trivial and innocent.

Georgia law requires an electoral audit of one race to ensure overall election integrity. The Republican secretary of state, who had ardently supported the president during the campaign, chose to audit the presidential race because of its national profile. Given the closeness of the results, several million votes needed auditing for statistical validity. The secretary of state decided to audit all five million votes. He didn't want to leave any doubts. And since each vote produced a paper ballot, he asked for a recount *by hand,* which also addressed the demands of the presidential campaign. Surely that would put fraud rumors to rest.

The recount found two major discrepancies, which is exactly why Georgia had the recount. Roughly 2,700 uncounted ballots were found on a memory card in Republican-run Fayette County. Those ballots netted 400 votes for the president. In heavily Republican Floyd County, the site of the Make America Great Again rally in Rome I attended just before the election, around 2,600 uncounted ballots were uncovered by the audit. Once counted, they yielded roughly 800 net votes for the president. The additional votes did little to close Joe Biden's 12,000-vote lead, however.

The hand recount functioned as intended, uncovering discrepancies and clearly proving the election had been fair; it's hard to dispute the paper trail. Georgia's Republican governor certified the election on November 20, thereby earning the ire of the president and many of his supporters.

The president's campaign requested a second recount and Georgia obliged. It, too, proved the election results were valid. The governor recertified the results.

In the end, the president lost Georgia three times. Still, people alleged widespread fraud.

The governor, the secretary of state, and I appealed to anyone inside or outside Georgia to bring forward evidence.

I personally vowed to chase the trail like a bloodhound.

The secretary of state's office investigated more than 250 allegations. The Georgia Bureau of Investigation assisted in investigating many of these. U.S. Attorney General Bill Barr even tasked the Department of Justice to investigate voter fraud in Georgia and other states.

These professional investigations discovered no wrongdoing outside isolated, inadvertent, or procedural errors. They found no malice, no conspiracy, nothing that would swing the election. Our dedicated local and state law enforcement teams performed their investigations with skill, honesty, and thoroughness. They found no evidence of fraud.

I chose to trust our law enforcement professionals.

On courthouse steps across Georgia, attorneys and plaintiffs backed by the president and GOP leaders promised overwhelming evidence that state and federal investigators had somehow missed or hidden.

I wasn't clear if they were calling law enforcement incompetent or corrupt. The answer was really neither.

Here's what's telling: Plaintiff attorneys wouldn't repeat in front of a judge what they so brashly told the public. They might lie for their clients *outside* the courtroom, but *inside* they didn't dare risk their license by lying to a seated judge or submitting false evidence.

In court, plaintiffs never presented anything admissible; law enforcement had in fact done their job well.

Despite our offers and pleas, no party leader nor any individual ever contacted my office or any other state office with actual evidence of voter fraud. There were some isolated irregularities reported as there are in every election, but nothing sinister and nothing sweeping.

No fraud.

Mostly, people just echoed what they heard their leaders saying. They repeated claims investigators had already disproven. I began to suspect if any fraud was occurring it was the false rumors being spread by leaders in my own party.

I began to refer to the president's claims as the Fraud Hoax.

★ ★ ★

Some of the most-repeated charges of the Fraud Hoax bear debunking one by one:

- **Dark of night:** *Election officials at a major polling location told observers to go home and then resumed counting ballots and committed fraud.* First, Georgia state law simply *allows* observers to be present during counting; they are not *required* to be present. Second, when officials began to pack up at 10:30 p.m., election observers voluntarily left before workers received instructions to

continue counting. Third, I don't believe election officials want to cheat, especially since a five-year prison
sentence can accompany election fraud.

- **Dead people:** *Significant numbers of dead people voted.*
  Just not true. Georgia's election procedures make this
  virtually impossible unless an inadvertent error stems
  from a deceased voter and active voter in the same
  precinct having the same name. Even that is unlikely.

- **Double count:** *Poll workers fed the same ballots into vote
  scanners multiple times.* First, voters fed their own ballots
  into machines. Second, the hand recount of paper
  ballots would have uncovered this type of fraud.

- **The Matrix:** *An algorithm in the state's new voting
  machines changed votes for the president to votes for Joe
  Biden.* Again, printed ballots provide an indisputable
  check here. The hand recount of all paper ballots cast
  in the election proved technology did not meddle with
  outcomes in Georgia.

- **Secret suitcases:** *Election workers unpacked suitcases of
  fake ballots and illegally counted them.* Fulton County
  election workers, some of whom had been working
  since 7 a.m., thought they could go home at 10 p.m.
  on election night. They stored ballots in official suitcases and sealed them for safekeeping until the next day.
  When they learned they were *not* going home, they
  unpacked the same suitcases and continued counting
  those same ballots. Every minute of this process is
  captured on video.

- **Watergate:** *A water line break damaged ballots and
  affected the results in Fulton County.* A toilet overflowed
  in one counting location. Workers moved all ballots

and equipment out of the way before any damage occurred and cleaned up the puddle.

- **Dominion:** *Several purveyors of election equipment and software engaged in an international conspiracy, directed by Venezuelan communists by some counts, to undercount ballots marked for the president and/or overcount those marked for former Vice President Biden.* The massive lawsuits filed by these companies against those making accusations of fraud are telling. Networks immediately began backpedaling and qualifying their statements to avoid (they hoped) paying the legal price for knowingly propagating misinformation. No credible evidence of any corporate conspiracy whatsoever has been uncovered in Georgia or elsewhere—nor has any admissible evidence been submitted by any plaintiff.

Plaintiffs and partisans promised to present mountains of evidence that would support these and other allegations. Instead, Georgians received mountains of misinformation from every direction possible: mail, social media, email, DMs, texts, voicemails. Many friends called me directly to ask about one of these bogeymen. I always patiently shared the facts I knew, but those of us in state government who understood the process were always playing catch-up. Political arsonists started false rumors that spread like wildfire—and much faster than more complex but truthful answers. Just like a wildfire leaves a scorched trail, lies that get into the public mind become hard to erase.

Sometimes it seemed Republican leaders wanted the president to win so badly they just preferred to believe the rumors or even worse, made them up themselves.

Hundreds of communications per hour poured into my digital accounts. Many came from longtime friends and fellow Republicans who've supported my campaigns. My standard response became, "Thank you for alerting me to this situation. Can you provide evidence or proof I can forward on to the secretary of state and his investigators?"

I have yet to receive a reply.

Brooke received similar messages. She responded the same way. Unlike me, she did get a response. It was very telling: "I don't have to prove it; somebody else does."

It wasn't a hard riddle to solve.

Those out for selfish purposes took possible scenarios and weaknesses in the electoral process and used them to create false narratives that they viciously spread. The problem was that many rumors felt like they *could* be true.

They just weren't.

And when these bad actors repeated the claims again and again, louder and louder, the claims did not become any truer. Yet the more people heard them repeated, the more people began wondering, "Well, *could* there be some truth to them?"

Then it got worse. Elected officials sensed many Republican voters beginning to believe the allegations and conspiracy theories irresponsible leaders and some media were relentlessly pushing. These representatives made a cold calculation. Each one evaluated his or her chances in the next election. "If I want to win reelection," each one asked, "can I afford to say Georgia held a fair election?" They thought "No" was the answer.

The president and his propaganda machine had them shaking in their boots and lying out loud.

These elected Republicans also asked, "If I don't want a primary challenge from the right, do I need to show my loyalty to the president by supporting his claims, even though I know in my heart the charges aren't true? And even though my responsibility is to speak truth to my constituents?"

Sadly, they decided on "Yes."

Behind closed doors, exasperated Republicans shared their frustration at the increasingly crazy and bizarre accusations. They'd confess they didn't believe the allegations. But then they'd shake their heads and tell me, "My voters are calling me nonstop about this, they're just convinced it happened. How can I contradict the president?"

A long list of people I formerly admired stood by quietly, tacitly supported the president's claims, or fanned the flames outright with more insinuation and misinformation. Sure, they were leaders in the president's Republican Party but they had a higher duty to the truth, to the Constitution, and to all Americans—they didn't just represent Republicans.

It distressed and saddened me to see my colleagues and fellow Republicans supporting what I'll call the most serious domestic attack on American democracy I've ever seen.

★ ★ ★

There was an election conspiracy in Georgia.

The *real* conspiracy involved leaders who irresponsibly spread untruths and rumors after the election, seeking to mislead honest Georgians and invalidate the people's fairly expressed will.

Now, I've never wanted a single illegal vote counted, and I want all election rules followed. I am supportive of any citizen pressing an election case through the legal system. So I supported the president's right to pursue legal avenues, even as I thought his vocal accusations were hurting his own case, the Republican Party brand, the GOP's chances in Georgia's upcoming U.S. Senate runoff, and democracy itself. One by one, his legal avenues closed in Georgia as state and federal judges, as well as justices of the Supreme Court, dismissed each case, including the following:

- **The Big One.** *The State of Georgia and three other states violated their own election laws, thus invalidating 20 million individual votes and 72 electoral votes.* The Supreme Court of the United States declined to hear the case.
- **The Deadline.** *Chatham County illegally counted ballots received after 7 p.m. on election night.* A Chatham County judge dismissed the case.
- **The "Kraken."** *Multiple individuals and groups committed widespread fraud, including rigging voting machines.* A federal judge in Georgia dismissed the case.
- **The Re-do.** *Thousands of isolated irregularities occurred, and more than 450,000 illegal votes were cast, invalidating all November 3, 2020, results and necessitating a new election.* Fulton County Superior Court and the Georgia Supreme Court both rejected the case.
- **The Signature:** *Georgia violated voters' rights by implementing signature matching procedures eight months before the election.* State and federal judges dismissed the case.

On a larger scale, courts rejected some 60-plus cases filed by the president and his allies across the country. No plaintiffs brought forth admissible evidence, although each promised they would. Untold dollars were spent by plaintiffs and defendants to litigate these cases. The final gasp of the 2020 election litigation onslaught came at the U.S. Supreme Court on March 8, 2021. The Court declined to hear the last of the president's election lawsuits. Fringe cases would still pop up, but the real legal saga had effectively ended.

The former president and his cohorts would have to find other ways to whip up the base and raise money.

Court cases and recounts confirmed no widespread fraud upended the 2020 election. Locally, they also confirmed 53.7 percent of Georgians legally and properly voted for a Republican state senator. Republicans held all but one congressional seat and no Democratic U.S. Senate candidate received a majority. The Georgia House and Senate remained firmly under Republican control.

As a Republican, those results don't appear fraudulent to me.

Still, it fascinated and frightened me how many Republicans who won their races on November 3 clamored to essentially invalidate their very own election. Of all the senselessness that would come, perhaps this one fact perplexed me the most: *Never once did I see a Republican who won their election question the results of any race other than the presidential election. How could their own election be valid but Joe Biden's election not be valid?*

I remember reading George Orwell's novel *1984* in high school. Big Brother, the dictator in the novel, employs something called "doublethink." It enabled him to have people simultaneously believe two contradictory things. Doublethink came to mind as I saw the president and his allies convincing people that the election was simultaneously riddled with fraud and wholly legitimate. Where Republicans won, the election was fair. Where they didn't, rampant fraud occurred.

Republican doublethink, aggressively pushed by leaders, social media, activist groups, and conservative media, assaulted good people's independently informed world views. Their campaign was shockingly successful. It quickly led to dangerous GOP groupthink. Months after the election, this mindset persists in our party.

The election-fraud conspiracy has come to be called the Big Lie.

My simple message to fellow Republicans?

Don't buy the lie.

★ ★ ★

Please remember I'm providing these explanations and perspectives as a lifelong Republican and conservative. I wanted our candidate to win, flawed as he was. I campaigned hard for him (although like many, I'd soon have some regrets about that).

I'm also the lieutenant governor of Georgia and I represent every voter in the state. Those voters chose the other guy in a free and fair election. Unlike pundits and plaintiffs, my fellow elected officials and I have a responsibility for governing. Georgia voters and the state constitution made Joe Biden the winner.

I also offer these points as a father of three boys who tries hard every day to teach them the value of truth and integrity. Adults—especially elected leaders—pushing falsehoods don't help me make my case. And I certainly don't want Parker, Bayler, and Ryder to catch me lying or defending false claims, particularly falsehoods related to something as important as an election.

Unfortunately for my Republican Party, it just seems roughly 12,000 more Georgians voted for former Vice President Joe Biden than for the sitting president.

Did I like the results? No.

Did I accept them? Yes.

That's how American democracy works.

The president and his followers operated under a different understanding, however, and that post-election hurricane they brewed settled right over my head.

2

★ ★ ★

DECEMBER 2020: IN THE CROSSHAIRS

A WEEK AFTER THE ELECTION, THE FIRST OF GEORGIA'S THREE presidential ballot counts ended. The secretary of state certified the election, but many accusations of fraud had yet to be fully debunked or investigated. I took these proliferating charges seriously because that was my job, and I just couldn't believe that so many elected officials—many of my own colleagues— would ever make up false stories.

Surely they had evidence that I hadn't seen.

CNN's Chris Cuomo interviewed me during this period and asked me if Joe Biden was president-elect. He caught me off-guard. I talked around the question. Virtually no Republican had yet acknowledged Biden as the winner, and I wasn't sure if I should be the first. I thought deeply about my response later that night.

As I'd told CNN already, I had not seen any evidence of fraud and I knew a recount wouldn't change the outcome. And while the party line had become, "We'll let the legal process play out," the cases I'd seen had no grounding in reality. They largely sought to disenfranchise large numbers of my constituents on shaky grounds. That didn't sit well with me.

Then someone sent me a screenshot of a Twitter statement I made in 2016 recognizing the president-elect not long after the election. They were right to hold me accountable.

You know what else I realized? Everyone with whom I'd been speaking had voted straight-ticket Republican. Sometimes our unconscious bubbles conspire against us. I always encourage people to step outside Republican echo chambers, yet there I was, sitting in one.

So I reflected hard on what I knew:

- Georgia officially reported 13,558 more votes for the Democratic ticket than the Republican one.
- 53.7 percent of Georgians voted for a Republican state senate candidate.
- Incumbent GOP U.S. Senate candidate David Perdue outperformed his challenger with 49.7 percent of the vote in the regular Senate election, but because that total was below 50 percent, he'd face a runoff in January.
- The candidate backed by the Democratic party in Georgia's U.S. Senate special election failed to receive 50 percent of the vote; he didn't win outright and would also face a runoff.
- Georgia Republicans held all their congressional seats except one, and that one loss didn't surprise anyone given the district's recent political shift.

- Neither the courts, the secretary of state's office, my office, the governor's office, nor law enforcement had discovered any widespread fraud or illegal procedures.
- The Republican secretary of state and his Republican-led elections division oversaw a procedurally sound election process under valid Georgia law.
- The people bringing charges of fraud generally had ulterior and selfish motives.

I knew Georgia's governor and secretary of state well; they were friends and partners in governing. In my role as president of the senate, I'd come to trust those elected and appointed officials who oversaw the election process; I'd met many of them as I traveled across the state. I had zero reason to believe massive fraud occurred in the state of Georgia under such competent Republican leadership and oversight. Additionally, being naturally analytical and having gone to an engineering school like Georgia Tech for three years, I'm a data guy—and I saw the data here.

Let's go ahead and call the data *facts*.

Also remember that throughout the fall, most polls showed Joe Biden ahead or tied with the president. The president outperformed many projections, which makes it even more unlikely someone committed massive fraud to help Joe Biden.

To believe widespread fraud occurred in Georgia, one would also have to believe the following:

- Perpetrators conducted a sprawling yet perfectly secret operation, duping our law enforcement, and leaving absolutely no evidence of their actions.

- The conspirators risked lengthy prison sentences for their efforts—yet only gave Biden a margin of 12,000 votes.
- While taking the extreme risk to commit systemic fraud, they didn't bother to help Democrats win in down ballot races. They allowed all but one GOP member of Congress to be reelected, and they didn't rig an outright victory for either Democratic U.S. Senate candidate—or both, which would have assuredly given Democrats control of the entire Senate.
- Conspirators recruited accomplices in a significant number of Georgia's 159 counties, and nobody detected or revealed any of their fraudulent actions.
- Numerous county, state, and federal judges rejected valid evidence of conspiracy and then conspired themselves to all rule against the president's campaign and its supporters.
- Pro-Biden conspirators outfoxed a modern Republican-run state election apparatus and hoodwinked multiple highly competent local, state, and federal law-enforcement agencies.
- Georgia law enforcement either missed the fraud ("They were incompetent") or conspired across agencies and jurisdictions to cover it up ("They were corrupt").

Republicans protesting the election have asked me to believe all of these, either individually or collectively. They have provided no evidence, and I continue to believe their groundless accusations are entirely absurd and indefensible.

Moreover, they're just plain sad.

The disrespect these propagators of misinformation showed to Georgia law enforcement is among the most disturbing aspects of their argument. Standing with law enforcement became a Republican cornerstone in 2020.

Until the president lost his election.

Suddenly, the party pivoted and effectively charged federal and state law-enforcement officials with incompetence or corruption.

Partisans say widespread fraud occurred. Therefore, law enforcement was either too dumb to find it or too corrupt to report it. Which was it?

In one post-election tweet the president called me "corrupt." Hey, he can hit me all he wants with falsehoods. But *nobody* should tar Georgia law enforcement with false and brazenly disrespectful labels like that, whether you say them directly or indirectly. For my part, I trust the men and women of law enforcement. I appreciate their hard work to secure our elections.

I apologize on behalf of my party for casting doubt on their good name.

Let me say this one more time: *Nobody has ever, still to this day, provided any credible evidence of voter fraud in Georgia.*

If election fraud had happened in Georgia, it would have been the most extensive, bipartisan, criminal, and brilliant conspiracy in U.S. history. That it remains undetected would prove the supreme genius of the Democratic perpetrators.

I just don't believe that scenario.

Nor do I believe a single one of the individual possibilities listed here.

The facts led me to conclude no widespread fraud had occurred.

Not a single thing indicated otherwise.

Georgia held a free and fair election amidst a surging pandemic.

Good for Georgia.

★ ★ ★

Some may believe politicians run polls and consult with experts before choosing from a breakfast menu. I assure you I have neither the staff, the money, nor the inclination to live or govern that way. When I told CNN I'd seen no evidence of voter fraud, I stopped short of acknowledging Joe Biden's victory.

I'm only human.

All I'd heard from fellow Republicans was "fraud" and even though nobody had produced evidence, a tiny part of me wanted to believe them. Remember, I had wanted the president to win.

And beyond that, really, who wants to be the first to step out of line?

Immediately after the interview, I got a gnawing feeling in my gut. "Come on, Geoff," my gut said. "You know the truth here. You need to tell it."

My gut was right but the politician in me looked around and saw virtually every Republican official and conservative pundit claiming the president had won and the Democrats had orchestrated a massive scheme to defraud America. These prominent figures, who many people trusted, were whipping up voters, dominating the media, and raking in dollars—lots of dollars from hardworking people they duped into believing lies so they could get their money. Not wanting to stop their gravy train, they attacked anyone who opposed their view.

Did I really want to stick my head up and have it snapped off? The honest answer is, "No, I didn't."

My trajectory had never been toward politics and certainly not toward politics in Georgia. My life began in Leechburg, a western Pennsylvania town so small it didn't have a hospital, so technically I was born fifteen miles away in New Kensington. My father left the U. S. Air Force as an airman first class and in western Pennsylvania, his job options were either a steel mill or a coal mine. He and my mother saw the discouraging future of those industries, and they decided he should earn a two-year degree and use his talents in sales. The plan worked. My dad landed a job.

As he began to climb the corporate ladder, my parents moved my sister and me to New Hampshire. He kept climbing and we kept moving, to Connecticut, to New Jersey, to Georgia, to California, to Illinois, and finally back to Georgia. My family had the unique pleasure of calling seven different states home. We were proud of Dad. But every new position he earned meant we had to load up the moving truck yet again.

My mother held our family together. Every time we moved, Dad would quickly resume his travels for work and Mom would set about making sure her son and daughter found new friends, but neither of us ever found a friend like our mother. My sister always made a few friends in school and excelled in the classroom. It's no surprise she became a standout teacher and school administrator here in Georgia.

Me? I found friends on the field.

Baseball and football became my home bases in every new town. I realized being among the best athletes on the field was a terrific way to make new friends. Maybe that's why I practiced so hard: Being the best athlete made being the new kid easier.

Team sports always attracted me, likely because that's where I found my friends. My teammates and I shared passion for sports and boyhood dreams of playing ball in college, maybe even the pros. In every town, these guys would inevitably become my closest companions—until our family moved again and I had to start all over. Team sports also gave me comfort and focus while so much else seems in flux. I always felt at home on a baseball diamond or football field.

The summer before my senior year in high school, we moved back to Georgia. My second day in the state found me in two-a-day football practices at Chattahoochee High School. That very first day I met Brooke Mize, one of the team's trainers—yes, the same Brooke who sat next to me at that chilly rally in Rome, Georgia. Shortly thereafter, I became the starting quarterback. I proved myself solidly average with an above-average arm. The baseball coach noticed and asked me to try pitching. Every game, more college scouts came to watch. There were more than twenty scouts at my last game; scholarship offers came in from across the country. One spring night I was scheduled to play third base. My coach found me before the game and said, "The Georgia Tech scout is here tonight. Do you want to pitch?"

I said, "Give me the ball."

I threw a nine-inning no hitter with seventeen strike-outs. The coach from Tech liked what he saw. That summer, I accepted his offer to attend Georgia Tech.

My first year at Tech, our team reached the finals of the College World Series. By my junior year, I'd proven myself a decidedly average pitcher, yet for some reason, I decided a pro team should draft me. I worked the phones just like my dad had as a salesman and the Florida Marlins—now the Miami

Marlins—drafted me in the 69th round. I was the 1,646th pick of the draft. They'd probably never picked that low.

Brooke and I got married and baseball became our lifestyle. In six seasons, I played for five teams as I moved up from rookie ball to AAA, one small step away from the Big Leagues. I added New York, Florida, Maine, Arizona, and Calgary, Canada, to my long list of homes; I lived in Illinois for a second time.

Worn-out shoulder ligaments unfortunately crushed my ultimate dream of playing for the Marlins on their home field. But how could I complain? I'd played pro baseball for five years with my wonderful wife supporting me. I was luckier than I deserved.

My baseball career ended, and we came home to Georgia, where I started my first business. In all those years, politics never crossed my mind. My dreams were baseball and family— and business, too, primarily to support the first two. I never aspired to duke it out over policy in the public arena.

That viewpoint hasn't really changed too much.

Look, I'm lieutenant governor of Georgia. My family and I hadn't signed up for full-time political life like the national-level folks. I fulfilled my duties at the capitol during each year's legislative session and then in large part returned to my role as a husband, dad, and community member. I liked raising my boys in peace. But how could I let them see me spreading rumors or lying to my constituents? What would they think if I compromised the democratic principles and institutions that they'd learned to revere in civics classes? What would it teach them if I stood by idly in this storm of misinformation?

Beyond that, how could I quietly let America's storied and principled conservative party become something my boys would never even consider joining?

If the Republican brand was being ruined—which is what seemed to be happening—what would happen to the conservative policies I truly, truly believe will give them and everyone else's children the best chance at prosperous and happy lives?

Not speaking up became less and less of an option.

I never wanted to be in this position, but there I was, an unlikely lieutenant governor smack in the middle of one of Georgia's—and America's—greatest modern crises.

I had a choice to make.

By the time my next media interview came, I felt completely comfortable doing what my pesky gut said was right. I stuck my head up. Even though it might end my career in politics, I did what I knew was right: I spoke up and told the truth.

At an industrial studio outside Atlanta, I sat down in a simple chair. A backdrop of downtown Atlanta hung behind me and a television camera faced me. I would eventually sit in that seat more than 60 times over the coming weeks as I explained Georgia's elections and America's politics to viewers in the U.S. and abroad.

It turns out potentially throwing away one's political career isn't natural for a body—it has a self-defense mechanism. My breathing suddenly became quick and shallow as the clock showed the interview getting closer.

I recognized the feeling. It reminded me of my days on the pitcher's mound when I found myself with a full count and runners on base.

I'd been here before.

★ ★ ★

Twenty-one years earlier, I had walked into the Florida Marlins locker room after being called up for a spring training game in 1999. I'd played with the squad before during spring training to fill a hole, but this time, they were really taking a look at me. From the bullpen, I watched the Marlins play the New York Mets for eight innings. I got the call late in the game and had time for literally one pitch to get loose.

First batter I faced got a hit. Second batter got a hit. Then I walked the third guy. Bases were loaded for Mets first baseman John Olerud—Johnny O—thirty years old (ancient to me) and holder of a record-setting contract. He'd set single-season Mets records the previous year with his batting average (.347) and on-base percentage (.447). He was the last guy I wanted to face in this situation. He was exactly who the Mets wanted at the plate.

Nobody was betting on me—just as no one was betting on me twenty-one years later when I walked into that studio in Atlanta.

A pitcher's mound can make a reliever in trouble very lonely, even amidst thousands of people. The mound gives him no place to hide. Bases loaded, no outs, and I'd wrestled Johnny O to a 3-2 count using a series of fastballs and sliders. Our veteran catcher Jorge Fábregas called for time and jogged out to the mound.

"Can you throw a 3-2 change-up?" he asked, wanting me to use my third-best pitch, which is a deceptive pitch that travels much slower that it looks.

"Why?"

"If you throw a fastball, he'll take your head off." He smiled.

"Okay, I'll throw a change-up."

Jorge nodded and jogged back to his spot behind the plate and squatted down. He gave the sign.

My breathing had become short and shallow. I was nervous. I collected myself and took the long deep breaths that had calmed and focused me during countless tight games before this one. I held the ball close to my chest and took one last breath. I reared back and delivered the pitch.

Johnny O popped the change-up as high into the sky as I'd ever seen one fly. The shortstop caught it.

One out. The next batter hit a 1-2 slider into a double play.

Three outs. Inning over. In the dugout, the Marlins' manager said, "Way to get it done, Duncan."

In baseball, it's all about throwing the right pitch when the time comes.

In that bare-bones Atlanta studio, facing the blank television camera, I took the deep breaths I'd taken on the mound years ago. I wasn't just facing a batter and a crowd of spring-break tourists, however. I was facing the nation, a suspicious Republican Party, and a very uncertain reaction.

This was what it felt like to—possibly—throw away a political career.

But just as I knew the change-up was the right pitch that day in spring training, I knew in my gut that stating the truth was the right choice in 2020.

I took a breath and threw the pitch.

★ ★ ★

In that next interview and others, I began acknowledging Joe Biden would be the next president of the United States. I began saying Joe Biden was president-elect or that come

January 20, he'd be our nation's chief executive. I probably never phrased it the same way, but I'd drawn my line. I stood firm that Georgia had held a free and fair election. I criticized the false allegations and misinformation flowing from political figures, including the president of the United States.

As the days went by, recounts, new information, and a continuing lack of evidence of fraud all strengthened my defense of Georgia's election integrity. I felt more and more confident in my position even though fellow Republicans made me feel like *I* was the crazy one. Most GOP leaders still claimed widespread fraud had tipped the election. They labeled any dissenters traitors and attacked on all fronts.

It's funny. The television camera doesn't react to what you say. Neither do cameramen—and even if they had reacted to my statements, I couldn't have seen their expressions because they all wore masks to protect against COVID-19.

Heck, I couldn't even see the anchors asking the questions. They were just voices in an earpiece. Consequently, my words echoed around my head and around the studio, then they faded away. It almost seemed unreal.

Many times during interviews in November and December 2020, I wondered, *Did I actually say that? Did anyone hear that?*

Then the interviews would end with a producer buzzing into my earpiece: "Thank you, Lt. Governor Duncan. We're clear," And it would be done.

A heavy door separated the room from the outside world and I knew what awaited me. Maybe if I just stayed in that dark room after each interview, there might be no consequences.

That wishful thought crossed my mind often.

Even though I was among the first GOP leaders to acknowledge Joe Biden's win, I felt entirely confident in my statements.

And really, I thought other leaders in Georgia and elsewhere would join me in accepting the results. Then we'd all move on as we always do after an election.

I wouldn't really be alone for long, right? Weren't others in my party seeing the same data and realities I was?

Well, I quickly discovered *plenty* were not seeing the same things.

My public positions triggered what would become a long-running stream of social media hate. My interviews put me on the president's radar in a bad way. Once he began attacking me, countless others whom I'd never met and who had probably never even visited Georgia unleashed tweets and posts that I doubt they'd show their family or friends. I certainly couldn't show them to my family.

At one point, I posted a picture of my fifteen-year-old son learning to drive. Even that drew hot responses: "Use that China Dominion money to get your son a new car!" Even some folks in my inner circle began backing away, realizing I wasn't playing around—I was seriously going to take aim at the party line.

I thought it was a ridiculous line to hold. In retrospect, it only seems more ridiculous.

Nobody had produced evidence of widespread fraud, and the election wasn't particularly close. Joe Biden had won an insurmountable margin of 74 electoral votes. He'd won the most popular votes in U.S. history: 81 million. That was 7 million more than the president, who had won the second-most popular votes in U.S. history.

Still, taking second place in a two-way race means you lose. In this case, the misguided life philosophy of racecar driver Ricky Bobby, from the movie *Talladega Nights*, actually applies: "If you're not first, you're last."

Moreover, acknowledging the winner has been what leaders of both parties have done in most every election cycle for nearly 250 years, even if their party loses. In Georgia, we did have experience with a Democratic candidate not conceding the governor's race in 2018. The most glaring exception to conceding was of course after the election of 1860, which gave America its first Republican president. An entire region seceded from the Union upon Abraham Lincoln's election, but they still didn't falsely cry "fraud" as did so many Republicans in 2020.

In 2020, a majority of Republican elected officials refused to acknowledge Joe Biden's victory in November and early December. They deliberately misled their trusting constituents. To please one person, they purposefully fanned the flames of misinformation or refrained from extinguishing them. I at least thought reason and patriotism would prevail once the Electoral College cast its votes.

Well, I've been wrong before and I was wrong then.

Nothing changed after the Electoral College officially cast its votes 306 to 232 for Joe Biden and Kamala Harris on December 14. Precious few Republicans leaders acknowledged Biden would be inaugurated on January 20. If others didn't say outright that Biden's election was illegitimate, they certainly used every means possible to imply it.

I've never seen politicians so scared of the truth—and that's saying a lot!

Through dogged repetition, unrelenting saturation, and conspiracy with local party officials, media and activist groups, the president's leading Republican allies managed to convince 75-plus percent of the party their lies were true.

★ ★ ★

As I write this months later, history is already being rewritten. Many will tell you they didn't spread misinformation. They'd say they were just concerned about what others were saying, or raising concerns for their constituents, or they were just reporting the news. I don't buy those excuses for a minute. It's like a representative publicly saying, "People are telling me voting machines changed votes and Democratic poll workers double-counted ballots. It sounds fishy but I'm not sure it's true yet." Or, "We're hearing reports of massive fraud in Georgia and that a major voting equipment manufacturer may be behind it." That is intentionally injecting falsehood into the dialogue. That's fanning the flames of misinformation.

To make everything trickier, Georgia's two U.S. Senate seats would be decided in a January 5 runoff. The nationwide results of the November 2020 election meant Georgia's two senate races would decide control of the *entire* U.S. Senate. If the Republican candidates lost, the Democrats would become the majority, due to Vice President Kamala Harris's tiebreaking vote.

So my mission and challenge after the November election became sharing the truth about Georgia's election *and* simultaneously doing all I could to help the two GOP candidates win their respective runoff elections. Too much rode on the runoff for me to get distracted by sideshows but that became an increasingly hard line to walk as election rigging became a central theme in the campaign—one that was *not* helping the two Republican candidates who were getting dragged into the mud.

The president and his surrogates continued fanning the flames, and they forced the two GOP senators into fringe and dishonest positions on election fraud. I worried their rhetoric would lose the race for our party. I walked the line as best I could and just kept repeating: "No fraud in November, trust the electoral system, vote in the run-off on January 5, and please, out-of-state politicians, stop making the GOP seem like an extreme faction. You'll only hurt our candidates in the run-off."

I felt at odds with this new prevailing dynamic. It reminded me how I felt looking over the crowd at the November 1 rally. I felt like a stranger.

Who was this party?

Why did it seem to literally worship the president?

What was it doing to the bedrock of our democratic republic?

What would it do to me?

Each time I said "No fraud" or "President-elect Biden" on national television, the insults and hate poured in from across Georgia and from forty-nine other states too.

Leaders of the Fraud Hoax had done their job well.

They had flooded every information channel with conspiracies spun to please their boss. Their boss should have been their constituents; sadly, it wasn't. People were helpless to resist the onslaught.

Groupthink—or doublethink—was the goal, and Republican leaders achieved it.

But every time I looked into that black camera lens and spoke my mind, I gained confidence in my voice and my path. Maybe it's just easier to say what needs saying when it's only you and a camera in a small dark studio room; you can feel like the outside world doesn't really exist.

That is, until tweets start pouring in, making your phone vibrate nonstop until you turn it off.

Each time I read messages on the way home, I sure felt glad I had two Georgia state troopers with me. People wanted to rip my head off. Friends disappeared or became rabid enemies overnight.

At best, fellow Republicans thought I'd lost my mind. At worst, they thought I'd become a traitor deserving of the traditional punishment.

I found myself on an island – one that was getting pounded by bombs and artillery. Still, I never—not even for a moment—regretted my decision.

Faith and family pulled me through.

★ ★ ★

My guiding Bible verse has always been Nehemiah 6:3: "I am doing a great work and I cannot come down." Nehemiah had come to Jerusalem to rebuild its crumbled wall and he did so in 52 days. Along the way, enemies tried to distract him and coax him down from the wall. He gave them the same response: "I am doing a great work and I cannot come down." He paid them no attention, he didn't stop his work, nor did he waver in his important mission. Nehemiah finished his task.

That verse carried me through an earlier political firestorm when I led the passage of Georgia's hate crimes bill.

Georgia had been one of only four states without such a law, and I believed Georgia should stand for what's right. Many in my party disagreed—some vehemently—but I stayed focused on doing a "great work" and we passed the legislation. I drew on Nehemiah again during the election's aftermath. His story reminded me protecting Georgia's integrity and guarding the votes of my constituents were too important for me to let distractions win.

Family also got me through the aftermath of the 2020 election. The five of us prayed together often at bedtime. We always felt my fight was the good fight. God bless them; they never left my side and never stopped supporting me. They never let me doubt my path. I can't express how much that meant when the entire state and national parties seemed set against me. My resolve occasionally wavered but they were always there reminding me what was most important. And to me, showing them how to stand up for the truth and what's right was more important than anything else.

One story stuck out. Years ago, my second son Bayler was going into middle school and his church small group had a father-son campfire one evening. The leader handed each dad a coaster and a pen. "Write your best advice for your son," he said.

He caught me completely off-guard. I looked at the coaster. I looked at Bayler, who was looking expectantly at me. Then out of nowhere came a phrase. I wrote it on the coaster: *"Doing the right thing will never be the wrong thing."*

Sometime after saying the phrase "President-elect Biden," which was still forbidden in Republican circles during December 2020, I was sitting at my desk at home getting pummeled on social media and conservative media by the president and everyone else.

"Bayler," I shouted.

From upstairs, I heard, "Yes?"

"Do you still have that coaster? The one we got at the small group campfire?"

"I think so."

"Will you bring it down here?"

When Bayler brought it into the office, I asked him to read it to me. *"Doing the right thing will never be the wrong thing,"* he read.

The words felt like aloe on sunburn.

Bayler almost never tweets, but he tweeted that quote from his account all on his own several hours later. I hit like and retweet. The tweet got hundreds of thousands of impressions and thousands of interactions.

It also created a firestorm in our house. Brooke was furious I'd retweeted Bayler because of what it might expose him to—and she was right. I talked with Bayler and he said, "Dad, I love it. *Doing the right thing will never be the wrong thing.*"

I knew we were on the right path. Law, fact, and truth were on our side. Eventually that'd be clear to everyone else too. Wouldn't it?

It certainly wasn't yet clear to the president, and he put me in his crosshairs.

Our relationship had begun much more auspiciously.

Several years earlier, when the president didn't know me from Adam's housecat, Brooke and I found ourselves riding with him and the First Lady in the Beast. The first thing the president asked me after the doors closed was, "Do you know you are riding in the most expensive vehicle in the world? Knock on that window."

I knocked. It felt nine-feet thick.

"You can shoot that window with an AK-47 72 times before it shatters."

"What happens on the 73rd shot," I asked.

"Don't worry," he said. "The Secret Service will have us covered up by then."

During our drive from the airport to downtown Atlanta, the glass was never tested and the president never stopped talking. He was informed, energetic, and talked policy as it related to Georgia. The First Lady was extremely engaging and would smartly prompt her husband from time to time.

During that first ride, people lined stretches of road and congregated at intersections; many brandished posters. My eyes saw mostly protestors and negative signs. The president turned his head and looked out the window into a group of maybe fifty protesters. He saw the lone person waving a blue flag emblazoned with his name. "Look, Melania," he said, "They love us in Georgia, they love us!"

I remain convinced he meant it. He only saw one person in the crowd.

We pulled into the underground garage at our destination. The president waved off the Secret Service so we could finish our conversation before he stepped out.

"You have a bright political future," he said just before opening the door. "You might be governor of Georgia one day. If you ever need my help, let me know."

Now, I'm sure he practiced that line on state-level officers like me in all fifty states. He likely forgot my name after taking two steps. I nevertheless appreciated the moment's sentiment. Moreover, he far exceeded my expectations. He was pleasant and upbeat. He had a surprising grasp of policy and how it related to Georgia. He and the First Lady seemed like a good team. I bet most people who met the guy I met in the limo would support him.

The guy on Twitter? Not so much.

Shortly after I began speaking up for the integrity of Georgia's election, he turned his Twitter account against me. He launched his uncivil barrage when I departed from the party line by speaking the unfortunate truth for Republicans. On national television, I continued to say, "President-elect Biden," followed by, "No evidence of election fraud."

Those two phrases were entirely true but not being spoken by Republican leaders solely because they feared the ire of their leader. It either never occurred to them or they never cared that they were misleading their constituents. There aren't many political offenses worse in my mind. They broke the sacred trust.

My previously warm relationship with the president crumbled as my path diverged from his. As he did to so many other allies, he turned on me at our first disagreement. You can imagine many people piled onto the president's attacks. You can also imagine quieter voices shared their support with me; many congratulated me for speaking the truth.

What?

How did we reach a point where anyone deserves special accolades because they *don't* lie or spread misinformation?

Who set our bar so low?

How are we explaining this to our children?

It saddened me that we'd reached this point.

We were in an uncivil war indeed.

★ ★ ★

I'd given the president's team every chance to prove their cases, to show me evidence that would overturn Georgia's election results.

Really, I asked again and again and again.

The evidence never came. But evidence never mattered to the president or his lieutenants. Truth conflicted with their narrative: *The president didn't lose and he's not a loser.*

Truth conflicted with his foot soldiers' aims too: Keeping power mattered more than keeping the Constitution. So these formerly responsible party leaders insisted the other side must have cheated.

Hey, I get it. I feel like that all the time watching the Georgia Bulldogs or Georgia Tech Yellow Jackets. I want my teams to win.

But blaming the umpires just doesn't work in business or government.

Like many before me, I was demoted from friend to foe in 100 characters. I was Twittered by the president. It turns out he didn't forget my name after all.

When Georgia's two recounts affirmed Joe Biden's victory, the president looked to Georgia's Republican-dominated General Assembly to save his presidency. Boldfaced, he asked the governor to call a special legislative session so the bicameral Republican majority could replace Biden electors with those loyal to him.

Let me be clear: *Georgia's constitution does not allow for that remedy.*

None of our constitutional officers would subvert our laws, no matter who was asking. The governor, secretary of state, and I are responsible to all of Georgia's nearly 11 million citizens, not just those who voted for us. We would respect the will of Georgia's voters, even if we campaigned for a different election outcome.

Republicans have traditionally been the constitutional-law party, the party of law and order. What would we become if we abandoned those principles?

The president apparently felt the answer was, "We'd be in power." Holding onto power had become all that seemed to matter.

When the governor, the Republican speaker of the house, and I all refused to support calling a special session, the president dialed up individual state senators and representatives to urge them to circumvent those of us holding the constitutional line. The entire legislature was conferencing in Athens, Georgia, at the time. While we were planning for the upcoming 2021 session, the president was trying to find elected Georgians willing to step across a constitutional line on his behalf.

Fortunately, our institutions held firm.

Throughout the post-election period, the president had continually attacked Georgia's governor, secretary of state, and me via Twitter. He laid into me with his best insults just weeks after praising me from the stage at his rally in Rome. I only replied once, very measuredly.

I simply thanked him for his four years and encouraged him to focus on the upcoming dual runoff election for Georgia's two U.S. Senate seats, a contest that would determine party control of the entire Senate.

Some people questioned why I didn't respond more often and in kind with sharper language. Well, one, nobody wins a Twitter war with a bully—you only get dragged deeper into the mud. And personal fights just aren't my thing.

Two, my parents raised me better than to respond in kind. In fact, they'd tell me to ignore the taunts altogether.

Three, my family and friends read my tweets and I believe my words matter, as does my example. What would a Twitter war teach my three boys?

And finally, I didn't want to distract from the approaching January 5 runoff, which our party needed to win in order to retain a majority in the U.S. Senate.

Names and threats didn't just come from the White House, however. My family and I were in unfamiliar territory. I was doing national television interviews, standing up for my state's integrity and my own—standing up for the Grand Old Party I thought America needed. The president was actively attacking me, and his followers readily took his cue.

Trust me, you don't want to read their comments and you especially don't want your children to read them.

Here's a particularly sad part. Occasionally I'd click on a profile of someone who'd savaged me. I'd read their personal description. I was shocked and saddened by the number of self-described mothers-of-four, Sunday-school teachers, proud grandparents, and church volunteers who lashed out with language and sentiments I won't repeat. Their leaders had failed them. The Republican figures they trusted intentionally misled them for selfish purposes. They fed them lies and whipped them into people those children, Sunday school students, grandchildren, and fellow church volunteers wouldn't recognize.

Shame on our party's peddlers of deceit and anger for what they did to good people.

Twitter wasn't the only avenue for political venom. Threats—many of which were actual physical threats—came in via my voicemail and email accounts too. Many came from folks I knew! People even went after Brooke.

Put yourself in my shoes for a moment. How would you feel? What would you do?

Every morning I'd wake up thinking I've been dreaming. Surely, I only dreamed fellow Republicans were sending us ominous threats. I must have imagined that nearly every official in my party saw election fraud where none existed. Then I'd look out my window. I'd see the added security posted by the Georgia State Patrol. My boys and I played catch in the front yard with troopers watching, making sure nobody hurt us because Dad simply told the truth.

Imagine explaining that to your children.

I also had to explain the security to our neighbors: "Sorry guys, I told the truth and decided not to overturn Georgia's election. Our neighborhood may be attacked by Republicans."

The neighbors had seen footage of protestors outside homes of other state officials in Georgia and elsewhere across the country. I'm sure they quietly wondered when mobs would arrive on our street.

But my neighbors stayed put. They supported Brooke and me. They'd bring the troopers coffee after long nights or early mornings. And those devoted troopers—whom I can't thank enough—were working twelve-hour shifts. Each of those acts heartened me. They also reminded me how quickly we'd gotten here. In just a few weeks, my world had flipped upside down. I went from party leader to party doormat.

The governor, secretary of state, and other elected officials received similar threats—from people who consider themselves Republicans! And it went further. A twenty-something employee of Dominion Voting Systems in Gwinnett

County, Georgia, received death threats simply for doing his job. Conspiracy theorists seized on a tidbit about this young contractor transferring data from an election management system to a county laptop so he could read it—a perfectly appropriate and normal part of his job. Those looking to sow misinformation distorted what he was doing (just his job), added colorful falsehoods and innuendo, and spread social media rumors that this young man had committed fraud, somehow manipulating data and helping the Biden campaign. The resulting rumor storm led to someone charging this innocent worker should be hung for treason. Others piled on.

Can you imagine how he felt?

These deceptive Republicans put innocent people in danger. Think how I felt about my constituents being endangered like that.

I'll say it again: *I am responsible for and responsible to every single Georgian, whether they voted for me or not.*

★ ★ ★

A nonsensical fissure arose in the Georgia GOP and in the national party too. Not acknowledging Joe Biden's election became a litmus test within the Republican Party. So did supporting conspiracy theories and claims of fraud, even those that had been debunked. And this was happening even though *months* after the election nobody had found evidence of fraud.

Even months after Joe Biden took the oath of office, accepting and spreading the Big Lie remained the GOP litmus test.

I'm sorry, but what kind of democratic and free-thinking political party makes affirming a falsehood its litmus test?

Is this the Republican Party we want?
Is this how our leaders try to win elections now?
Is this a route to a national majority?
We *must* be better than this.

3

* * *

JANUARY 2021: TWO RUNOFFS AND A RANSACKING

AFTER NEARLY TWO MONTHS OF ATTACKING GEORGIA'S Republican leaders from afar, the president and his administration resorted to hand-to-hand combat. On January 2, 2021, the president of the United States rang up Georgia Secretary of State Brad Raffensperger and asked him to flip the election.

As background, Brad was a Republican who'd been a strong supporter of the president and had broad support within Georgia's GOP before the 2020 election. The party liked Brad and Brad worked hard for the party. Perhaps that's why the president thought he might be receptive.

The now-infamous call lasted 62 minutes and the president spoke for 73 percent of the time. Twice, he talked for more than ten minutes uninterrupted. He said 7,102 words; Brad said just 540. The president rambled through nearly every conspiracy theory I'd heard, each one of which had been debunked many times over. If you listen to the recording, the monologues themselves are cringeworthy. You can hear the president of the United States sharing roughly forty minutes worth of misinformation.

I'm sure none of his advisors had recommended he make the call.

Nevertheless, he did.

Secretary of State Brad Raffensperger picked up the line around 3 p.m. on Saturday, January 2, 2021. The president dove right in, saying, "Hello Brad and Ryan [Ryan Germany, general counsel to Georgia's secretary of state, who was also on the line] and everybody. We appreciate the time and the call. So we've spent a lot of time on this and if we could just go over some of the numbers, I think it's pretty clear that we won. We won very substantially in Georgia. You even see it by rally size, frankly. We'd be getting 25 [to] 30,000 people a rally and the competition would get less than 100 people. And it never made sense."

That set the tone. The president began a long soliloquy, noting he won by "hundreds of thousands of votes" and peppering Brad with debunked fraud allegations. These were all rumors we'd heard before. Georgia law enforcement had investigated and found these accounts were, in fact, nothing more than rumors.

Like I've said, many *sounded* like they could be true, but when investigated, they just weren't.

Brad held his ground against the presidential onslaught. "Well, I listened to what the president has just said," Brad responded to all those on the call. "We've had several lawsuits and we've had to respond in court to the lawsuits and the contentions. We don't agree that you have won."

That lit the president's fuse. Here's a little of the back-and-forth from the call transcript. Imagine yourself in the shoes of the Georgia secretary of state and his general counsel.

THE PRESIDENT: I won this election by hundreds of thousands of votes. There's no way I lost Georgia. There's no way. We won by hundreds of thousands of votes. I'm just going by small numbers, when you add them up, they're many times the 11,000 [roughly Biden's margin of victory]. But I won that state by hundreds of thousands of votes. Do you think it's possible that they shredded ballots in Fulton County? Because that's what the rumor is. And also that Dominion took out machines. That Dominion is really moving fast to get rid of their, uh, machinery. Do you know anything about that? Because that's illegal.

RYAN GERMANY: No, Dominion has not moved any machinery out of Fulton County.

THE PRESIDENT: But have they moved the inner parts of the machines and replaced them with other parts?

RYAN GERMANY: No.

THE PRESIDENT: Are you sure, Ryan?

RYAN GERMANY: I'm sure. I'm sure, Mr. President.

THE PRESIDENT: What about, what about the ballots. The shredding of the ballots. Have they been shredding ballots?

RYAN GERMANY: The only investigation that we have into that—they have not been shredding any ballots. There was an issue in Cobb County where they were doing normal office shredding, getting rid of old stuff, and we investigated that. But this is stuff from, you know, from you know past elections.

THE PRESIDENT: It doesn't pass the smell test because we hear they're shredding thousands and thousands of ballots, and now what they're saying, "Oh, we're just cleaning up the office." You know.

BRAD RAFFENSPERGER: Mr. President, the problem you have with social media, they—people can say anything.

THE PRESIDENT: Oh this isn't social media. This is Trump media. It's not social media. It's really not; it's not social media. I don't care about social media. I couldn't care less. Social media is Big Tech. Big Tech is on your side, you know. I don't even know why you have a side because you should want to have an accurate election. And you're a Republican.

BRAD RAFFENSPERGER: We believe that we do have an accurate election.

THE PRESIDENT: No, no you don't. No, no you don't. You don't have. Not even close. You're off by hundreds of thousands of votes.

The exchange continued like this, with the president throwing rumor after false rumor at our secretary of state. The president finally paused, and Brad responded, "Well Mr. President, the challenge that you have is, the data you have is wrong."

To his credit—and unlike many Republican leaders—Brad Raffensperger didn't bend to the president's will. He stood up for truth and for Georgia and for the Republican Party I know.

The president's strategies all failed to move Secretary of State Brad Raffensperger to action. Unfortunately for his own cause, the president was dealing in rumors, not facts. He just could not accept he'd lost Georgia by 11,799 votes. He seemed bizarrely and utterly convinced he'd won. In part, this was due to all the people around him telling him what he wanted to hear: "Yes, sir. There was massive fraud. You didn't really lose."

One more price of dishonesty. One more price of lost backbone and personal integrity.

Finally, the president said, "So look. All I want to do is this. I just want to find 11,780 votes, which is one more than we [need]. Because we won the state."

He continued.

THE PRESIDENT: And flipping the state is a great testament to our country because, you know, this is—it's a testament that they can admit to a mistake or whatever you want to call it. If it was a mistake, I don't know. A lot of people think it wasn't a mistake. It was much more criminal than that. But it's a big problem in Georgia, and it's not a problem that's going away. I mean, you know, it's not a problem that's going away.

RYAN GERMANY: This is Ryan. We're looking into every one of those things that you mentioned.

THE PRESIDENT: Good. But if you find it, you've got to say it, Ryan.

RYAN GERMANY: Let me tell you what we are seeing. What we're seeing is not at all what you're describing. These are investigators from our office, these are investigators from GBI [Georgia Bureau of Investigation], and they're looking, and they're good. And that's not what they're seeing. And we'll keep looking, at all these things.

THE PRESIDENT: Well, you better check on the ballots because they are shredding ballots, Ryan. I'm just telling you, Ryan. They're shredding ballots. And you

should look at that very carefully. Because that's so
illegal. You know, you may not even believe it because
it's so bad. But they're shredding ballots because they
think we're going to eventually get there ... because
we'll eventually get into Fulton. In my opinion, it's
never too late. ... So, that's the story. Look, we need
only 11,000 votes. We have far more than that as it
stands now. We'll have more and more.

Later, he went at the secretary of state again, raising the
specter of the January 5 U.S. Senate runoff, just three days away.

THE PRESIDENT: Well, under the law you're not allowed to
give faulty election results, okay? You're not allowed
to do that. And that's what you done. This is a faulty
election result. And honestly, this should go very fast.
You should meet [with my attorneys] tomorrow because
you have a big election coming up and because of what
you've done to the president—you know, the people
of Georgia know that this was a scam. And because of
what you've done to the president, a lot of people aren't
going out to vote and a lot of Republicans are going
to vote negative because they hate what you did to the
president. Okay? They hate it. And they're going to
vote. And you would be respected. Really respected, if
this thing could be straightened out before the election.
You have a big election coming up on Tuesday. And
therefore I think that it is really important that you meet
tomorrow and work out on these numbers. Because I
know Brad that if you think we're right, I think you're
going to say, and I'm not looking to blame anybody.
I'm just saying you know, and, you know, under new

counts, and under uh, new views, of the election results, we won the election. You know? It's very simple. We won the election. As the governors of major states and the surrounding states said, "There is no way you lost Georgia." As the Georgia politicians say, "There is no way you lost Georgia." Nobody. Everyone knows I won it by hundreds of thousands of votes. But I'll tell you it's going to have a big impact on Tuesday if you guys don't get this thing straightened out fast.

He closed the call with this: "We just want the truth. It's simple. And everyone's going to look very good if the truth comes out. It's okay. It takes a little while but let the truth come out. And the real truth is I won by 400,000 votes. At least. That's the real truth."

Those are the words from the transcript. I wanted you to see what Georgia was up against and how we held the line. I wanted you to see what misinformation spread by Republican leaders had wrought.

It's also worth noting that in late December, the president called the Georgia secretary of state's top fraud investigator, Frances Watson, who was conducting an audit of mail-in ballots in suburban Cobb County. The president hoped her investigation might identify significant discrepancies and void a large number of mail-in ballots, which tended to skew Democratic in our 2020 election. Again, mail-in ballots typically don't give advantage to one party or another. But in Georgia in 2020, the president's vocal yet baseless campaign against using mail-in ballots disproportionately led Republicans to vote in person. Investigator Watson knew where the presidential phone call was leading and to her credit, she stood firm.

She said to the president, "I can assure you that our team and the [Georgia Bureau of Investigation], that we are only interested in the truth and finding the information that is based on the facts."

The president reminded her, "You have the most important job in the country." Then he explained, "When the right answer comes out you'll be praised....People will say, 'Great!' Because that's what it's about: the ability to check and make it right. Because everyone knows it's wrong."

The president reminded Ms. Watson of his winning margins in nearby states, but it didn't matter how many votes he got in Alabama, Florida, or South Carolina. He didn't get as many as Joe Biden did in Georgia.

Despite his claims that "everyone" knew he'd won by sizable margins in Georgia, neither Ms. Watson nor anyone else found stashes of missing ballots or the fraud the president alleged.

★ ★ ★

The president's fixation on Georgia got even more sinister, as events of the next day showed.

In December, Jeffrey Clark, the formerly unassuming acting head of the Department of Justice's civil division, shocked his colleagues by drafting a letter for the DOJ to send to Georgia state legislators to ask them to void Joe Biden's win. The letter claimed—and this was an outright lie—that the DOJ was investigating voter fraud in Georgia.

Remember, the DOJ had already investigated fraud allegations in Georgia and found no evidence.

Accordingly, Acting Attorney General Jeffrey Rosen rejected Clark's proposed letter. The letter was the real fraud, not the election.

Yet undeterred by truth, the law, or the acting AG, Clark then apparently convinced the president to replace Rosen with himself!

As later investigations and sources revealed, Rosen had already resisted significant pressure to investigate Georgia from the president's chief of staff, Mark Meadows. Meadows violated long-standing rules separating federal investigations from White House influence and sent no less than five emails to Rosen, pushing him to investigate debunked fraud theories in Georgia and elsewhere. Rosen refused Meadow's requests as he had Clark's.

These events culminated in a contentious White House meeting on January 3, the day after the president called Brad Raffensperger.

Democracy hung in the balance while the president spent three hours debating whether to replace Rosen and use the DOJ as a personal tool to overturn Georgia's election.

Ultimately, the only thing that kept the president from replacing Rosen was likely the united threat to resign made by Rosen's Department of Justice leadership team.

The president's reluctant decision not to remove Rosen effectively ended Meadows' meddling and stopped yet another executive plot to use the Georgia legislature to void our state's sovereign election results and cancel the votes of more than 2 million of my constituents.

The president finally ceased interfering in Georgia's affairs.

We had come that close to an even greater crisis.

★ ★ ★

For a moment, play out the entire election fraud scenario with me.

Pretend the Department of Justice had sent that letter to Georgia legislators or the president had empowered a new acting attorney general (Jeffrey Clark) to intervene in another way.

Imagine if Georgia's secretary of state had conjured up 11,780 ballots for the president.

What if Georgia hadn't rebuffed the president's request to call a special session of the General Assembly?

What if the governor and I responded to the president's tweets and used our pulpits to beat the drum and ensure Republican electors replaced Democratic electors? Maybe we would have used as our reason the 11,780 votes our secretary of state would have "found" after succumbing to presidential pressure on that infamous January 3 phone call.

What if Georgia had in fact overturned the fairly expressed will of Georgia voters and changed the presidential election results as many Republican leaders so badly wanted?

First, I'd have lost all moral authority when talking to my constituents. Perhaps worse, I'd have lost all moral authority in my own house. I would have gone against everything I promised my family I'd stand for. Moral authority up in smoke.

Likewise, our state party and most of its elected officials would have lost their moral authority too. For what?

Walk several steps further with me.

Assume Georgia Republicans essentially threw out the 2,473,633 votes cast for Joe Biden and Kamala Harris. We would have pointed to voter fraud as our reason, although we couldn't have offered any proof.

Can you imagine how the millions of Georgians who voted for Joe Biden would have responded? The marches and protests would have made the 2020 racial justice protests look like picnics and July 4 parades. Counterprotesters would have countermarched.

Instead of rioting at the U.S. Capitol, many partisan supporters would have joined counterprotests in Georgia.

We'd have deployed state law enforcement. The numbers of protestors would have likely overwhelmed them.

Someone would have pushed too far.

People would have been hurt and almost certainly killed.

We would have opened Pandora's Box.

Georgia would have burned.

During those trying days in December and January, I kept running out this scenario in my mind. I just couldn't see how it would end without massive protests and likely violence.

Maybe I was being too dramatic, but I don't think so.

Keep going with me.

What if the president had then successfully overturned elections in several other states?

Say the Michigan leaders he invited to the White House had agreed to intervene and created a constitutional crisis that surely would have split their state.

Say the Department of Justice had somehow intervened in Pennsylvania, as DOJ bad actors and the president had considered doing in Georgia.

What if Arizona's Republican-controlled senate had conducted its own vote audit before January 20 as they'd wanted and changed the state's results to match their preferences?

What if one conservative on Wisconsin's Supreme Court hadn't stood up for principle and the state had voided 220,000 votes from two Democratic-learning counties, giving the state to the president?

Protests and counterprotests would have (very rightfully) erupted in those states too.

They would have burned alongside Georgia.

Certainly, protests would have taken place across the country. Would they have grown so large or violent that the president would have invoked the Insurrection Act to order National Guardsmen and U.S. troops to suppress the unrest? Would they have complied?

Would some officers and soldiers have turned on others?

Even if the Supreme Court ruled Georgia's actions unconstitutional and the Democratic-controlled House of Representatives protested, neither has any tools of enforcement. The president would have remained in the White House, and I would have remained in Georgia's State Capitol unless protesters carried us out—unlikely since law enforcement reported to us.

I'm reminded of President Andrew Jackson's callous quote upon hearing the Supreme Court had issued a decision deeming his mass removal of Native Americans unconstitutional: "Let them enforce it."

What would have happened to our country?

After nearly 250 years of vibrancy, American democracy would have collapsed in two months.

How would Republicans have felt afterwards? Really, ask yourselves that question and sit with it. I think we would have traded democracy for a despot, just so we could say "we won."

Our children's great American birthright is our democratic republic and its promise of fairness, opportunity, and freedom.

I believe the regret of cashiering our children's inheritance would be painful, lasting, and devastating.

Blood would have almost certainly been shed.

Martial law would likely have existed for months and possibly years as the man in the White House held onto his position.

No? Remember, he actually weighed a suggestion to have the military rerun elections in key states like mine.

Going forward, elections would be decided by those—or the one—holding power, not those voting.

Republicans would have ended the great American experiment.

★ ★ ★

Nobody talks about the logical conclusion of the Fraud Hoax. It understandably makes us uncomfortable. We saw a glimpse of that conclusion on January 6, 2020, at the U.S. Capitol.

Make no mistake: *If Republicans had overturned valid election results, the country could have collapsed.*

And everyone making false allegations and trampling the Constitution would have been complicit.

Look, I don't believe anyone wanted to see the republic crumble, but those supporting the Fraud Hoax were happy to score political points while others did the hard thankless work of saving that republic for them.

People accused Georgia of running elections like a Third World country. I'd argue the Third World shenanigans came from the vocal leaders who advocated overthrowing democracy.

★ ★ ★

The Fraud Hoax boulder continued rolling downhill and it bounced right on top of Georgia's January 5, 2021, dual U.S. Senate runoff election, where both our state's two GOP U.S. senators were up for reelection.

Long before the 2020 election, in December 2019, Georgia's longtime public servant Johnny Isakson resigned his U.S. Senate seat to concentrate on his fight with Parkinson's disease. Governor Brian Kemp defied the president and a vocal wing of the GOP when he nominated businesswoman Kelly Loeffler to fill Senator Isakson's seat until a November 2020 special election. The governor liked her as a successful suburban Republican with rural roots. The president's loyalist who wanted the job felt snubbed and immediately launched a challenge to Loeffler. The president refrained from supporting either candidate.

I suspected a sitting Republican president not endorsing a sitting Republican senator would have bad consequences.

It did.

Loeffler and her opponent spent 2020 trying to outflank each other on the right. Much like the president, they both sacrificed the middle for the wing. The reasonable positions and tone that had earned Loeffler the seat vanished by the fall. She fell in line with the president.

Less than a year after going to Washington, DC, her politics had shifted considerably. She ultimately managed to win enough votes in the November 3 general election to make the January 5, 2021, runoff election against a Democratic opponent endorsed early by Barack Obama. Only after Kelly Loeffler beat the Republican candidate the president *really* wanted did the president finally endorse her.

And when he came to Georgia to campaign during the runoffs, the president scarcely mentioned her name. Nor did he say much about the other Republican U.S. senator running for reelection, David Perdue. The president talked almost exclusively about election fraud. He insinuated the January 5 runoff would be as corrupt as the November 3 general election. He railed against the governor, the secretary of state, and me. He repeated the same mix of accusations and pointed to the same vague conspiracy theories.

Again and again, I encouraged the president and the party to stop fixating on false allegations of fraud and get our two incumbent Republican senators across the finish line. I knew the lies, anger, and vilification could lose the runoff for both GOP candidates; they were essentially convincing their own voters to stay home! If you saw any of my interviews, I always tempered my comments and tried to shift focus away from the inappropriate actions of the president and his supporters (although I never let them off the hook) and toward the upcoming runoff.

If both incumbents lost, Republicans would lose control of the U.S. Senate.

Thus all eyes fell on Georgia and money poured into these two races. All totaled, a record-shattering $937 million was spent on our two U.S. Senate elections. We Georgians appreciated the economic stimulus (even as we quickly tired of the ads).

In the end, Republicans lost both of Georgia's U.S. Senate seats by margins of 55,000 and 93,000 votes; the president had only lost Georgia by roughly 12,000.

I am *convinced* the party's tone and fixation on election-related sideshows cost Republicans these two seats and with them, control of the U.S. Senate.

Under this president, the GOP had lost the House, the White House, and now the Senate. The last president to accomplish this disappointing feat? Herbert Hoover in 1932.

The party's tone and message failed.

Pundits and media quickly blamed the Georgia loss on Republicans—and their leader—who fueled the Fraud Hoax, and I think that's a correct although not entirely complete assessment. But the media often overlooked the story of the third Republican candidate on the runoff ballot: the one who won. Georgians disaffected by national GOP nonsense voted out two Republican senators, but they still wanted a conservative in charge of the state's Public Service Commission.

January 5 was a politically momentous day. Until January 6 eclipsed it.

★ ★ ★

When all of us were young, our parents and teachers taught us that actions have consequences. Sometimes they're immediate. If you hit a baseball inside a house enough times, it's going through a window. Window breaks, parents dispense punishment, and you can't play baseball inside again.

Sometimes consequences come later. If you lie to your parents about the broken window or what you did the previous night, you may avoid consequences in the near term. But as the lies compound, your web gets tangled. Parents inevitably discover the truth, you've made the situation (and punishment) much worse than it was originally, and you've broken a sacred trust in the process.

The near-term consequences of Republicans crying fraud after the 2020 election seemed positive on one level: The president's PACs and related organizations raised more than $250 million in the weeks immediately after the election. The dollars came as they promoted fantasies they knew to be untrue. They begged dollars to fight fraud in the courts. They convinced good people—good, honest, trusting people—that they'd been fooled by Democrats, who had stolen—*stolen!*— the 2020 election from the president (but from nobody else on the ballot). To make it right, folks just needed to donate $10, $50, $100, or more.

In reality, these unscrupulous Republican leaders were tricking good conservatives and good party members who trusted them. They took people's hard-earned money and padded their own war chests without an ounce of shame. At last reporting, less than $10 million of that enormous $250 million haul went to overturning the election.

It turns my stomach. I hope it turns yours too.

Elected officials and also-rans from past elections found the spotlight. The more bombastic and outrageous their accusations, the more attention they often drew, the more money they conned out of good people's pockets, the more these tricksters advanced their selfish aims. "Maybe if I whip people up about fraud, I can finally win, maybe I can hold on, maybe I can get back in the game."

The more GOP leaders and influencers could ignore the reality of their national loss and lay blame on something other than themselves, the better.

Repeating a lie won't ever make it true. Yet at the time Joe Biden took the presidential oath, the incessant drumbeat of fraud accusations and conspiracies had convinced (depending on which poll you read) around 30 percent of Americans that he had not won legitimately. Roughly 75 percent of

Republicans believed fraud had tipped the election against their man. Nearly half of Republicans thought Trump bore no responsibility for the Capitol Hill riot.

Those were the sad consequences of a culture of deceit, of Republican leaders telling their party members Democrats had cheated, of leaders prizing victory more than principle. That's what happens when an entire party tries to delegitimize the vote. (Although just the presidential vote. I'll keep saying these folks never questioned their own election or other down-ballot GOP wins—it's doublethink, pure and simple.)

These Republicans succeeded in driving the partisan wedge deeper into America. And each one of them knew better. Every one of them knew they were misleading their constituents so they could advance themselves politically. I'd be fascinated to know how they explained their words and actions to their families.

They put politics over policy.

They put politics over people.

I hope their constituents discover the truth.

★ ★ ★

As I realized the Fraud Hoax wasn't ending, I began to see severe longer-term consequences. The Republicans who alleged fraud began to subvert the very core principles that have, in my mind at least, always defined the Grand Old Party. Many Republicans willingly shoved aside truth and the Constitution to get a win they didn't earn. They wrongfully incited our party's members.

One by one, four longstanding GOP pillars gave way to the blind pursuit of victory. Those pillars included states' rights, family values, an independent conservative judiciary, and the rule of law. Let's look at how the Fraud Hoax attacked each one of the four:

States' rights. World War II hero and Republican U.S. Senator Bob Dole always carried the words of the 10th Amendment on a notecard in his pocket. The amendment reads: "The powers not delegated to the United States by the Constitution, nor prohibited by it to the States, are reserved to the States respectively, or to the people."

Those reserved powers include elections.

Yet the Republican attorney general of Texas, supported by the Republican president, 17 Republican attorneys general in other states, and 126 of 196 Republican members of the House of Representatives, sued Georgia, Pennsylvania, Michigan, and Wisconsin for violating their own sovereign election laws.

Both of Georgia's then-U.S. senators, seven of our congressmen, and 28 Georgia state representatives supported these suits. They wanted to invalidate their own constituents' votes and strip their own state of its sovereignty!

The Supreme Court refused to hear the case and I thought the GOP's sudden assault on states' rights would end.

Nope. Seven Republican senators and 138 house members continued fanning the flames of misinformation and assaulting the principle of states' rights by objecting to the Electoral College count on January 6, 2021.

I noticed their careful wording. They overtly tried to claim principle while covertly taking sledgehammers to democracy's pillars. Some pointed to the doubt existing among the public.

Hearing that, I almost shouted into the television: "You created the doubt in the first place!"

These elected leaders continued propagating lies and baseless doubt. Oh, and they were raising money all the while: "Help me fight fraud!" Several U.S. senators sent fundraising solicitations to Georgians, promising to fight fraud in Georgia from afar if good Georgians could just send them $10, $50, $100, or more. This band of senators and representatives essentially voted to discount more than 10 million ballots legally cast by American citizens in elections fairly run by sovereign states dutifully exercising their responsibilities under the Tenth Amendment.

Outsiders, and unfortunately Georgia officials, too, tried to deceive my nearly 11 million statewide constituents, take their money, and scrap their votes.

I wasn't having it.

I am still furious.

Family values. Decades ago, Republicans became known as the party of traditional values such as family, faith, and character. Millions of people driven by faith became part of the GOP, bringing their worldview to Republican politics. Brooke and I count ourselves in that faith-driven community, and we see our perspective as important to the party's future. We want a family-friendly party whose members and policies reinforce the lessons we teach our children.

Yet many of the party's officials have sacrificed the moral high ground. They sat down when Americans needed them to stand up for basic values. Americans needed their leadership, and it didn't come. Instead, in order to win an election, they created false narratives, then pushed them or allowed them to spread. They trafficked in misinformation. They bore false witness.

If my boys did what they did, I'd call it lying.

False rumors sparked death threats and protests at officials' private homes. The same rumors ultimately led to seven deaths and hundreds of arrests related to the U.S. Capitol riot.

How can Republican leaders continue to excuse this behavior and allow such damage to our brand?

As early as 2016, I heard concerns from many friends about the president's indiscretions, language, bullying, and tendency to blur the truth. Brooke and I struggled to explain the president to our children. It makes it difficult to model moral behavior for kids when the most visible figure in the country gives daily lessons in behavior that runs counter to everything we try to teach: honesty, respect for others, kindness, respect for institutions.

Across four years, many of those friends who'd been shocked at first fell silent. They just accepted a "values vacuum" as the price of Republican control. They assumed this was the only way our party could win and save America from the other side.

Pray at church and consider Jesus's point of view on Sunday morning, but resume the unrestrained warfare against the other side right after the benediction: "All's fair in war and politics; God will look the other way because he's really on our side."

Nothing exemplified this better than when force was used to clear protestors from Lafayette Park before the president and his leadership—including the attorney general, secretary of defense, national security advisor, and chairman of the Joint Chiefs (who later apologized)—walked to St. John's Episcopal Church so the president could be photographed holding a Bible. Not his Bible, but *a* Bible, as he clarified.

Acts like those and four years of needlessly cruel and crude comments were some of the 1,000 cuts that sliced into the president's support and chipped away at the GOP's foundation as a party of family values.

An independent conservative judiciary. The administration placed three justices on the Supreme Court and 220 judges on the federal bench. The president and the Senate majority leader picked and confirmed these men and women because of their intellect and conservative views. They were not judicial activists. They based their opinions on a strict interpretation of, and respect for, the Constitution. They could be trusted to support Republican priorities.

By the way, I believe judicial appointments might be the administration's most important legacy.

Yet after the 2020 election, the president asked courts to take extraordinary measures to change election results and invalidate millions of ballots. He wanted them to sidestep the Constitution or contort its original intent—to be activists, to make law instead of interpret it. Or interpret it his way. He insulted his own conservative judges when they rejected or ruled against lawsuits he filed or others filed on his behalf.

The system of checks and balances conceived by the Framers and embedded in the Constitution worked, despite a siege by the executive branch. The independent judiciary upheld the law when other branches of government sought to circumvent it.

A conservative judiciary saved America from a conservative party that took pursuit of victory too far.

Let me add a warning. In March 2021, Republicans in Tennessee's state legislature sponsored legislation to remove a

Republican-appointed judge for ruling to allow more people to vote by absentee ballot in the 2020 election. It seems to me those state legislators are defining conservative judges as judges that rule how they'd like at a particular moment, and that an unpopular legal decision warrants removal of a sitting judge. Do Republicans want conservative jurists or jurists that vote how the president or a state legislature demands? It seems increasingly like the latter.

These politicians would forgo the long-established principle of supporting conservative jurists because they now prefer *pliable* jurists. Do we really want to start down this path?

That would wreck—*wreck*—the concept of an independent judiciary.

That is not what the Constitution intended, that is not conservative, and it's a path upon which no Republican should take a single step. It subverts the rule of constitutional law and undermines the balance of power among our government's branches. Has our party decided to place person and victory above conservative principle?

Rule of law. I like to think the Republican Party has always put the Constitution first. Republican representatives are the ones who speak most often about the rule of law. Republican presidents are the ones who appoint judges most likely to uphold the original meaning of our sacred founding document. Republicans have always supported law enforcement at all levels. Especially during 2020, the party's leaders praised police as they condemned violence sparked by bad actors in the nationwide social-justice protests—and let me emphasize the term "bad actors." I certainly supported the right of citizens to peacefully protest and raise awareness of injustice, which was what the movement did, and I think did very successfully. In fact, I worked my tail off to pass overwhelming bipartisan hate crimes legislation in Georgia during the summer of 2020. I'm proud we responded so forcefully to injustice and bigotry in our state. I only wish Georgia had acted sooner.

Despite railing against demonstrators that summer, the president and his allies called for unrest and demonstrations to overturn the election in the weeks following the November 3 election. Protesters and conservative activists threatened violence while the president's GOP stayed quiet. Nobody was standing up for law enforcement. The president himself pressured Republican leaders in Georgia, Michigan, Pennsylvania, and Arizona to flip election results through illegal means not allowed by their state constitutions. He called Michigan lawmakers to the White House. He called Georgia's governor and secretary of state. He threatened all of us on Twitter.

Perhaps the craziest aspects of these events? News media in the United States and abroad began referring to "attempts to overturn the election" and people just accepted that was, in fact, the president's aim.

Was this America or some dictatorship?

Rule of law?

The president and his enablers stoked his base with misinformation for two months—more when you consider he made election-rigging charges throughout his campaign.

Heck, he even claimed massive fraud in 2016—when he won!

He claimed he would have won the 2016 popular vote (which he lost by roughly 3 million votes) had millions of illegal immigrants not voted. But remember that the subsequent investigative committee he formed discovered absolutely no evidence of fraud and the committee quietly disbanded.

It's also worth noting a close associate of the president, Roger Stone, started the "Stop the Steal" website in April 2016. Making charges of election rigging was a cornerstone strategy for the president's two campaigns. He planned to cry "Fraud!" whether it happened or not.

The 2020 fraud hoaxers converted each court loss or other tactical defeat into further evidence of the vast conspiracy arrayed against the president and his followers. Each defeat became a rallying point for those wanting to "Stop the Steal." Even after the states certified their elections, every legal appeal had played out, and the Electoral College itself had voted, the standard GOP line remained, "The election was rigged."

As kids, we all learned what happens when you play with matches.

Two months of misinformation from political arsonists created a tinderbox. On January 6, 2021, a shameful gang of Senate and House Republicans added lighter fluid when they rejected Electoral College votes from sovereign states.

Then the president struck the match.

The GOP's reputation as the party of law and order shattered like the windows of the U.S. Capitol.

Maybe these developments shouldn't have surprised me. From my office inside the Georgia State Capitol, I could avoid getting tangled in Washington sideshows and instead focus on good state policy. Still, I saw the party drifting from its principled moorings. I saw the rancor growing.

Like other Republicans, I now wonder if I could have responded to the president differently as I saw him reshaping the national party into one where winning for winning's sake mattered more than truth or principle. One deaf to many struggling Americans. One whose divisive tone revved the president's base but alienated millions of hardworking citizens.

I'll live with the regret of not speaking up louder and earlier.

Perhaps because too many of us avoided the fight for too long, the GOP became a party willing to overturn a fair election because its candidate lost.

It became a machine that controlled local and national members alike, tolerating no dissent.

It valued winning above principle. It jeopardized conservative policies and democracy itself.

It lost a presidential election by 7 million votes.

★ ★ ★

In the aftermath of the January 6 riot at the U.S. Capitol, an armed escort walked me into the Georgia State Capitol each morning. I'd look out my office window and see armed men in combat gear standing guard in winter rain and cold, protecting the Capitol and me—and Georgia's democracy itself—from followers of the president identifying themselves as his Republicans. One by one, in just two months, and for one man's benefit, the Republican Party had toppled its most long-standing pillars.

After the Capitol riots and the inauguration of President Joe Biden on January 20, 2021, I thought Republican leaders would have had enough. Surely, they wouldn't drag the party into any more public controversies.

I gave them too much credit.

The next month, the Georgia GOP began to debate to election reform. Depending on your point of view, Georgia

Republicans aimed to fix real problems that emerged in Georgia's 2020 election, restore voter confidence that they themselves had undermined, or fix the system to give Republicans an advantage. Regardless of the legislators' true motivation, the fallout from the 2020 election landed Georgia and me in the national spotlight yet again.

Would this nightmare ever end?

4

★ ★ ★

FEBRUARY–APRIL 2021: CHAOS CONTINUES

I spent my childhood on sports fields. And I remember spring days when I'd want nothing more than to play outside, but rain kept falling. To me—an eager kid with a ball and glove—it seemed like the rain would never stop. Every time the downpour would lighten, my sprits would rise. "It's almost over," I'd think. Then, like Mother Nature was purposely taunting me, the rain began falling even harder. It always seemed as if the deluge would never end, and I'd never get to play ball.

As a lieutenant governor anxious to make real progress for my constituents as 2020 came to a close, I felt the exact same way. All I wanted to do was work on good policy, but the political storm unleashed by the 2020 election just wouldn't stop. It began with an embarrassing and preventable loss in November followed by false claims of fraud that led to attempts to corrupt local and state officials. Then came the loss of the U.S. Senate and a riot at the Capitol. The chaos kept going, like some runaway boulder tumbling down a mountainside.

When Joe Biden at last took the oath of office, I hoped the rain had stopped. Not that I believed President Biden himself offered a great hope for the country—I think his policies will take us in the wrong direction. I just thought his inauguration would mark the end of the Fraud Hoax and its fallout.

I thought with a new president in office and the old president off Twitter, the storm surge created by the 2020 election and the former president's misinformation campaign would finally recede.

I thought, surely, GOP leaders would end their preoccupation with fraud and falsehood, stop damaging the party's brand, and start helping real people solve real problems.

So what did Republican leaders do in early 2021? They didn't work on better policy or better tone. They didn't work on better understanding voters. They didn't learn from our loss.

They reached for an easier lever to pull: *election reform*.

Our secretary of state reported the 2020 election was Georgia's most secure election ever. Chris Krebs, the respected Georgia native who led the administration's cybersecurity agency, reported the 2020 election was America's most secure election ever. No evidence of significant voter fraud ever surfaced, and he said so, contradicting his boss. The president fired him.

We can always improve our elections, but we should be proud of our states and country for conducting a fair election amidst a pandemic and record turnout. Still, many people lost trust in the system. How could we restore confidence by making it harder to cheat and easier to vote? How could we address concerns of Democrats and Republicans about access and process?

That question preoccupied many Republicans when the 2021 legislative session began. Unfortunately, many held to the theory that if more people vote, Republicans will lose.

Is that true? No. But the former president and other leaders convinced many in our party that it *is* true.

Here's what's really true: If our party wants a future where it can win majorities and pass conservative legislation, it needs ideas and policies that can capture the hearts and minds of a majority, no matter how many people vote.

Because they got scared, GOP leaders became too focused on making voting more difficult. One of the former president's prominent supporters—a longtime Georgia congressman— attacked our Republican secretary of state, questioning why he was "working so hard to add drop boxes and take other steps to make it harder for Republicans to win."

To that I'd say, maybe the former president's GOP can't win when more people vote, but the GOP I envision sure can.

Bring on the voters. GOP 2.0 will win ever bigger.

★ ★ ★

As states began their legislative sessions, more than 250 election-related bills were filed across the country. Many were filed by Republican representatives as reactions to the GOP headliner losing the 2020 election, so right there, our party lost all credibility on election reform. We had a clear motive and selfish aims. Nobody thought GOP efforts were anything more than attempts to ensure more Republicans won next time.

I can say that numerous Georgia election bills were introduced by Democrats. Both parties recognized the system's flaws. We had brand-new technology in our polling locations. Our state went from processing 230,000 absentee ballots in 2018 to processing 1.3 million in 2020. We went from fewer than 4 million voters to more than 5 million. (And I want to see 6 million voters next time.)

Those changes tested our system and both parties saw ways to make it better.

I'm particularly proud that in the Georgia Senate, we put forth a package of four election reform bills on February 23, 2021, that passed with varying degrees of bipartisan support, from unanimous to just one Democrat. I had several Democratic senators in my office before the vote telling me they'd support the bills, but their caucus leadership was putting too much pressure on them to vote "No."

I called the bills "common sense election reform," and opted to use a scalpel instead of a chainsaw by putting forth four bills instead an overstuffed omnibus bill where you couldn't separate the good from the bad. Each of the senate's four bills improved the system without disenfranchising voters.

Collectively, these four bills would have allowed counties to begin processing absentee ballots before election day; shortened the deadline for counties to certify elections; asked for a written ID number when applying for an absentee ballot (and we were working on a provision for those without an ID simply to supply a birth year and the last four digits of a Social Security number); and make counties post the total number of votes that had been received—including in-person, early, and absentee votes—when polls closed on election nights. It was pretty good legislation, but I was still disappointed more Democratic colleagues didn't join us. That's politics.

Democratic leaders and activists just wouldn't let their senators work with Republicans on GOP-sponsored election bills, so peeling off individual senators was difficult, even when they'd tell me they agreed with the provisions in the bills.

Months ago, Democratic leaders and interest groups planned their narrative, and the content of bills really didn't matter. The left wing of the Democratic Party was going to equate any election reform with voter suppression. The Democrats' talking points and tone never changed from the introduction of the worst bills to the final vote on the final version, which would come at the end of the session, despite the elimination of the overwhelming majority of issues they'd originally complained about.

I get it, but it was still disappointing.

It reminded me of the difficult road to unity. It also reminded me how the GOP played right into the far left's hands. The party fell for their trap by rushing ahead with election reform and pushing bad ideas after we'd lost all credibility on the issue.

Like its out-of-office leader, the GOP just couldn't help itself.

I at least thought our Georgia Senate had offered a bright spot. We'd set a national example by passing bipartisan election reform that would increase election integrity, efficiency, and transparency.

A win for Georgia, right?

The win turned out to be fleeting.

A few weeks later, as expected, another election reform bill surfaced in the senate. It had only Republican support and would, among other things, eliminate no-excuse absentee voting (mail-in voting) for people under age 65 and limit weekend voting. State House Republicans introduced their version of the bill at the same time. It included several provisions with which I was uncomfortable, including severely limiting Sunday voting.

The House and Senate bills seemed to go out of their way to punish Secretary of State Brad Raffensperger for not flipping the election. All he was guilty of was being the former president's scapegoat, but in these bills, Georgia Republicans stripped their fellow party member of his chairmanship of the State Election Commission and implemented measures that gave the commission more power, which in turn gave the GOP-controlled legislature more power.

I felt the new bills made it harder for my constituents to vote—not just harder to cheat, as proponents said. It also played childish politics. It was a vehicle to let senators and representatives pander to the right fringe by including restrictive measures. Some members who supported these elements quietly told me, "We're just getting it on record for our base. It'll never make the final version of the bill."

Well, it got on record all right. They gave their opponents the exact narrative they wanted and that defined the entire debate.

Some supporters of the new bill also claimed it would boost voter confidence. Yes, but didn't voter confidence in elections fall because of the misinformation they themselves spread? Come on, nobody should get credit for purposely creating a crisis then swooping in with a solution.

And in this case, my fellow Republicans were swooping in with a solution in search of a problem. Georgia does not have a fraud issue.

I pushed back hard. The bill wasn't acceptable.

You know I like data points and I found it interesting that in April 2020, 76 percent of Americans thought all voters should be able to request an absentee ballot. I have very conservative friends who were livid—*flat out furious!*—that their fellow Georgia Republicans were trying to take away their option to vote by mail. People in both parties just like the convenience of voting by mail. And I'll add that Republicans passed the original bill to allow no-excuse absentee voting back in 2005, the year they claimed majorities in the legislature after decades of Democratic control. At the time, Democrats protested that voting by mail would be ripe for fraud.

How times change.

One more fact made repealing no-excuse voting by mail in 2021 problematic: more Republican women are voting by mail now than ever before—and women represent a critical voting block that's already slipping away from the GOP.

What if legislators had shown some real empathy and imagined being a working mother with responsibilities at work and home—and not having several hours to spend waiting in line to vote on Election Day, when lines would be even longer than in 2020 since so few people could vote by mail under their proposed bill. Are we making life easier or harder for them? Are we endearing ourselves to them or alienating them?

You know the answer.

Let's expand the tent, people, not shrink it.

★ ★ ★

As debate on this new, more restrictive election reform bill became increasingly intense, I began to feel mighty lonely

holding the gavel in the Georgia Senate. I'd stated my opposition to bills that made it harder for people to vote. By now
you know I put policy over politics, so you understand where
my heart was on this issue. This was clearly politics over policy.
I lobbied senators hard to derail the train. Still, I fell one
Republican vote shy of stopping the bill (SB 241) by keeping
it bottled in a committee.

I don't get a yes or no vote as president of the senate, so
after stating my case and urging my fellow Republicans to vote
down this bad bill, I passed the gavel to the president pro tem
and left the chamber.

I refused to preside over a bill with which I disagreed so
strongly.

Sitting in my office near the senate chamber, I had this
heavy feeling that Republican legislators just gave up hope that
our ideas could win elections. Their support of restrictive or
superfluous measures tells me our party no longer believes in
itself. If that's the case, the Democrats have already won and
we're laying down our arms because conservatism has lost. I'm
sure the philosophical surrender of today's GOP would leave
Ronald Reagan, with his boundless optimism and 17-million-
vote 1984 victory, shaking his head next to St. Peter.

It was also clear most Republican leaders missed any lessons
the 2020 election might have offered about tone, inclusivity, or
paying attention to real people's real problems instead of sideshows. If the loss of the White House and Senate didn't wake
anyone up, I don't know what will. And after all that, the GOP
let election reform steal energy and attention from legislation
that could really help Georgians facing real challenges.

I felt sad for my party and state because this crazy path
would ensure those conservative principles I love would

gradually erode as Republicans continued this self-inflicted decline. Democrats would gain more majorities and Georgians and Americans would pay the price as bad government-heavy policies replaced good conservative ones. I wallowed in that for a long time as debate proceeded next door. It was a bad emotional place to be for anyone, especially a conservative like me.

The pro tem gaveled the vote closed on the afternoon of March 8, 2021. The bill I had opposed, SB 241, which included strict limits on absentee voting and Sunday voting, passed 29–20. The bill then went to the Georgia House of Representatives for consideration.

Thankfully, I know how to lose. I learned to take my lumps as a pitcher. If I lost a game, my pitching coach and I would talk it over and he'd help me hit the reset button. I'd come out in the next game ready to win.

The bill wasn't yet final, so I went back to work. I hoped to change it as the legislative process played out. Remember, the House had to pass a version of the bill and then both House and Senate had to agree on a final version. There was still time to make it better.

Thankfully, cooler heads prevailed during negotiations—to an extent. The House and Senate wisely stripped out the most contentions elements of the bill including the repeal of no-excuse absentee voting and the limitations on Sunday early voting. Those were the Big Two, which most concerned Democrats and which most concerned me. Sadly, including them in the original bill defined the entire conversation.

I still didn't like some provisions that remained, like punishing Secretary of State Brad Raffensperger. I thought banning non-election workers from providing food and water to voters waiting in line was tone deaf. The left didn't like measures that secured ballot drop boxes and shortened the timeframe for absentee ballot applications.

Opponents of the legislation certainly didn't mention the bill expanded early voting options, and they didn't talk about Democratic ideas in the bill such as beginning absentee ballot processing before election day and posting total votes cast in a precinct at the time polls close.

Instead of giving a dissertation on each element of Georgia's election reform bill, I'll just say it made some procedural changes that we needed while also containing elements that weren't necessary. Nobody thought the bill was perfect, but it wasn't a monster. Yet the left never changed its talking points. And since almost nobody actually read the bill, those talking points were held up as gospel by people who'd never set foot in Georgia. Unfortunately, those talking points were far from the truth.

When asked to appear with the governor and other leaders for the bill signing on March 25, 2021, I demurred. I just didn't feel comfortable standing behind something I didn't enthusiastically support. That evening, the press began seizing on the image of our governor signing the bill in private and they used it to add fuel to their fire.

That wasn't the only story from the bill signing. A Democratic state representative tried to interrupt the ceremony as a protest. Now, I'm all for expressing dissent—I certainly did during this process. The representative continued knocking on the governor's closed door after state troopers asked her repeatedly to stop and warned her she'd be arrested. She continued her protest and the troopers arrested her, just as they would have arrested me or anyone else in that situation. It's security protocol, and they followed it to the letter.

I respect the representative's passion and willingness to be arrested because of it. She surely knew what would happen if she didn't obey the officers' directions, and, hey, sometimes that's how change is made. While the charges were dropped, the image remained. Unfortunately, the troopers on duty at the governor's office at the time were white and the representative was Black and so one more negative visual came to portray the election reform debate in Georgia.

It's still unsettling to me that a law enforcement officer doing his job is viewed in a negative light.

Look, I understand why the country turned its attention to Georgia's new law. And I still didn't like everything in the final bill, but here's the thing: *Nobody ever likes everything in a bill.* That's the legislative process.

But the train had left the station. It didn't matter what came out of Georgia's General Assembly—the far left was going to cry "Suppression!" They wanted to raise money off election reform just as the far right raised money by crying "Fraud!"

Well, cry "Suppression!" they did.

They pressured Georgia companies to condemn the bill. Here's a good example of how the situation spiraled toward ridiculousness. Delta Air Lines representatives had been engaged as the legislation was developed. Like me, they opposed the provisions that clearly made it hard to vote. When those measures were stripped from the final bill, Delta CEO Ed Bastian said the bill had "improved."

That was true. Especially from my perspective, the bill had improved significantly. Elements that might be considered truly suppressive were stripped out. Mr. Bastian had issued a completely reasonable statement, and one that reflected process more than outcome.

The far left wouldn't stand for that, however. They already had written their narrative—and they weren't going to change it, even if the realities changed. They attacked Delta and its respected CEO. A #BoycottDelta hashtag began circulating and so-called activists threatened to cancel out a very respected company that does a heck-of-a-lot of good throughout America and around the world. People wanted to boycott a leading Atlanta employer and hurt its thousands of hardworking employees because of one sentence that was, in fact, true.

Several days later, Delta's CEO issued a new statement condemning Georgia's bill. Under pressure, other companies issued similar statements and the narrative spiraled away from reality. Everybody knew it but nobody could say it.

I don't use Barack Obama as an example often, but it's appropriate to note how he has called out cancellers as fake activists who irrationally demand purity from everyone on every issue. The world and its people are imperfect, the two-term former president explained. If you want to make a difference, put your hands where your mouth is and get to work. If you just want to make a point, keep cancelling.

Republicans in the Georgia House of Representatives decided to cancel Delta right back. On the last day of session, they passed an amendment that would revoke a jet fuel tax break worth tens of millions of dollars to Delta. The amendment made it to the Senate, and I made sure it didn't see the light of day or receive a vote. The amendment wasn't tax policy, it was pure politics.

Amazingly, the boulder kept tumbling downhill.

★ ★ ★

The port of Savannah near Georgia's Atlantic coast is among the country's oldest ports. I'll proudly add that it now ranks among America's top five busiest. The Port of New York and New Jersey is the only East Coast port that handles more cargo—and they use two states to do it.

Like many port towns in the 1700s and 1800s, Savannah could be a dangerous place, especially for seamen. Ships couldn't sail without enough hands aboard so merchant companies and locals got into the shady business of finding volunteers, so to speak. By various unscrupulous and illegal means, agents would trick or force men to serve on long voyages. A man might drink too much or be beaten near-senseless one night and then find himself on a boat sailing east into the vast Atlantic when he came to the next morning—someone would have signed him up as ship's crew. There he'd be: railroaded into a bad situation from which there was no turning back.

That's exactly what happened to Major League Baseball in April 2021.

Misinformation swirled about Georgia's election reform bill and the uproar grew. The narrative pumped out by opposing activists spread quickly and soon, the misinformation conned President Biden himself into repeating false statements such as the bill would end voting hours at 5 o'clock. That wasn't true at all, but it fed the flames. Soon, Georgians really got burnt. Atlanta lost the July 2021 MLB All-Star Game.

After discussions with members of the Players Association and Players Alliance among others, Major League Baseball commissioner Robert Manfred worried the misinformation and politics would lead players to boycott the upcoming July 13 All-Star Game scheduled for Atlanta, where baseball would honor Atlanta's Hank Aaron, the home run king who'd recently passed away. Voting rights groups turned up the pressure on the commissioner. In a matter of days, he caved. He didn't explain the nuances of the much-improved bill or correct the inaccurate narrative. Instead, he decided to move the All-Star Game out of Atlanta.

I love baseball and Georgia too much to let that decision go unchallenged. What if, I wondered, we could use the game as an opportunity for MLB to make a real difference instead of a political point? I envisioned an alternative: keeping the All Start Game in Atlanta and holding a voter registration drive the week of the game. Hey, the MLB could host voting drives all around the country in Black, Latino, and every other community. This would give MLB players concerned about Georgia's voting laws the ability to do something about it while they were in town. That seemed like a win-win solution.

Well, the commissioner was under too much pressure to act reasonably. The voices in his ear wanted to punish Georgia and raise money on a wedge issue more than they wanted to sign up voters. Too late, he realized the situation had spun out of control. Like those unlucky sailors bamboozled into crewing 18th-century merchant ships out of Savannah, the commissioner was stuck. My compromise idea could never gain the necessary traction and I knew the fight was over.

In the end, the far left raised money off misinformation and outrage. The far right raised money off misinformation and outrage. Baseball and Georgia got crossways. And the good folks in the middle bore the brunt again. All because too many organizations and special interests were more interested in making a point than a difference.

All because people didn't put policy over politics.

★ ★ ★

I like to mention I have no natural political instincts. That seemed to be self-evident to most Georgia Republicans in the spring of 2021. In the six months since the election, I'd very publicly butted heads with party leadership over allegations of election fraud, over support for the former president, over conduct of runoff campaigns, and now over election reform. The press was speculating about the impending end of my political career. The usual suspects were circling, wondering if they could oust me and take the senate gavel for themselves.

For once, many Georgia Republicans and Democrats agreed: *What in the world is Geoff Duncan thinking?*

I'd left people on both sides of the aisle scratching their heads. A March *Atlanta Journal-Constitution* article was headlined, "The Curious Case of Lt. Gov. Geoff Duncan."

"Most elected Georgia Republicans are either cozying up to [the former president] or trying to avoid his wrath," the article began. "Not Lt. Gov. Geoff Duncan, who has set himself on a head-on collision course with the former president that's raising questions about his own political future." When the article mentioned my political future, it wasn't with optimism.

"The curious case of Geoff Duncan" should never have been that curious. If this were 2014, my case wouldn't be curious at all. In fact, there wouldn't even be a case.

Like nearly every other lieutenant governor in Georgia history, I did my best to campaign for our Republican senators at the state and national levels. I campaigned hard for my party's nominee for president. I rooted for my team to win. When nearly all of our state senators won reelection, I celebrated (remember, 53.7 percent of Georgians voted for a

Republican state senator). When the party's headliner—the president—lost, I was disappointed. Like other lieutenant governors, I triple-checked to make sure our elections ran free and fair; they did. Like my predecessors, I recognized one of my team members lost. I studied the loss and moved on to fight again next cycle. Nothing unusual there.

Of course, other Republicans didn't follow tradition in 2020. They took a bizarre turn and created an alternative universe where facts, truth, conservative principles, and institutional respect didn't matter. They followed a demagogue with a magical grip over their voters like rats followed the Pied Piper (it didn't end well for the rats, if you remember the story). Republican leaders let the truth be trampled or trampled it themselves. They intentionally misled their constituents and spread misinformation for personal gain on a scale never seen in American elections. They convinced millions of Republicans they were right; they made *me* look like the crazy one.

Now *that* is a "curious case."

Is it hard to understand that a husband and father of three boys chose to stick by the truth? That a conservative stood up for the rule of law? That a lieutenant governor did his duty and followed the traditions that have kept American democracy vibrant for nearly 250 years? That I made choices to do what's right? Has the former president poisoned our system to the degree that *I'm* the curiosity?

Apparently yes because everyone now expects Republicans to sacrifice every principle to satisfy one person. I'm here to tell you I'm not sacrificing a thing to placate the former president.

I will not worship him.

I will not excuse his excesses.

I won't believe his lies.

I won't mimic his tone.

I won't disingenuously pander to voters he's misinformed.

And I most certainly won't mislead my constituents because he wants me to.

He can hit me all he wants.

After all, I never planned to be in politics anyway. Yes, I love being able to fight for constituents from my statewide platform but holding onto the office isn't worth cashiering my principles or my family's respect. I can be plenty happy back in the private sector.

I thought Georgia journalist Jay Bookman framed this dilemma particularly well when he wrote, "When we ask why Duncan is [taking these stands against GOP leadership], it strikes me that we're asking the wrong question of the wrong people. Instead of wondering why Duncan is saying such things, we ought to be wondering why most of his fellow Republicans are not."

The election-reform fights of Georgia's 2021 legislative session confirmed our party is becoming even more lost, like a ship pulled into a hurricane, surrounded by rain and darkness and riding heaving seas. The captain and crew who plotted the course cannot lead us out. They don't know the way. They don't know how.

Maybe they don't even want to rescue us because they prefer the chaos.

I get that the passengers want to believe these officers know the way out—we all want to look up to our leaders. But friends, here on deck, everyone is soaked to the bone and the ship is taking on water. Someone else must take the helm before we go under; a new crew must step in and steer us out of this mess before it's too late.

At present, few party leaders are stepping forward to take the spinning wheel and level with the people. So entirely by default, I find myself looking at the helm and thinking about those words on my son Bayler's coaster: *"Doing the right thing will never be the wrong thing."*

I admit it: I'm not the best person to carry this banner. I had an itinerant education at three high schools in three states, followed by three years at Georgia Tech that earned me a last-round draft pick and no diploma. I wasn't supposed to be the Republican nominee for lieutenant governor. I never learned how to be a politician. In fact, an opponent criticized me for precisely that during the election-reform debacle—I took it as a compliment. I don't have a national following, a political pedigree, or deep pockets.

I always seem to be an underdog scrapping to hang on.

But I do hang on.

★ ★ ★

So maybe I can bring something to the table after all: I don't stop fighting for what I believe in. I won't be intimidated, especially when I stand on a rock of truth. I spent six seasons playing baseball in America's small towns and cities with teammates from every background who were dealing with every challenge you can imagine—real people with real problems. I pitched my heart out for them every night and I never wanted to let them down. I came to appreciate their many views on life and America.

Nobody believes in conservative principles more than I do. Nobody will fight for them harder. Using a moderate and reasoned tone doesn't mean you're not fighting hard—I like to think it means you're fighting with better arguments. I'm confident conservative solutions can work for Americans at all levels. I'm certain the GOP 2.0 movement, with its better Conservative **P**olicy, Genuine **E**mpathy, and **R**espectful **T**one, will expand our party's tent and win big elections. I'm convinced the Grand Old Party and the conservative movement desperately need healing and the ointment isn't coming from Mar-a-Lago or the usual partisans in Washington, DC.

The six nightmarish months after the election only strengthened my beliefs. Going through the fire clarified the right way forward and gave me the determination to pursue it.

I see a better path for Republicans and those who believe in limited government, personal freedom, a secure country, and a growing economy. And I see a better path for people who simply want a calmer, happier, more dignified, more unified, and more prosperous America.

Let me share that better vision with you.

PART TWO

A BETTER MESSAGE

*I emerged from the fallout of the 2020 presidential
election with a renewed optimism in the Republican
Party's future. Why? Because in all the confusion
and haze of those tumultuous and very difficult six
months, I glimpsed the clues and lessons that can
restore the party—and grow the party—if we're
wise enough to listen and brave enough to act.*

5

★ ★ ★

PIVOT POINT

In my second season with the Florida Marlins farm system, I played with the Kane County Cougars. I'd gone to one of my three high schools in nearby Naperville, Illinois, and my love for baseball really caught fire in those stands as a high schooler watching Cougar games. I used to dream about what it might be like to play for them one day.

Several years later, my dreams had come true, and I found myself on that field. Unfortunately, the story wasn't going as I'd envisioned.

After my first spring training, I barely made the roster for the Cougars. When I got there, I pitched terribly for the entire first month. It seemed like I never got an out. I felt like I gave up runs every time I went to the mound. I was sitting on the bubble of being released.

The situation had become outright precarious by the time my then-fiancée Brooke Mize flew up from Atlanta to see me pitch in a Saturday afternoon game. She watched me load the bases; I had runners on first, second, and third and a left-handed batter stepped into the box—not the guy a right-handed pitcher wants to face. I hurled a fastball at him and heard that crack.

I'd pitched long enough to know the sound: It was a home run.

I didn't even turn around. I just stared at the catcher as the guy ran out of the box and started his trip around the bases. The stadium was so quiet you could hear someone pop open a soda can.

About four seconds later, the home crowd starts yelling and screaming. Hey, maybe the ball didn't make it out! I turned around and saw the ball trickling out of the Wendy's Million Dollar Mitt, a big blow-up mitt on top of a scissor lift that was so far from home plate, I'd never seen any sluggers even get close to hitting it.

At that moment, I had never been that low.

To this day, and as far as I know, the ball I pitched was the only ball ever to hit the Wendy's Million Dollar Mitt. Here's the funny thing: The batter circled the bases yelling out, "Show me the money!" He's thinking he just won $1 million. I'm thinking he just won $1 million—and I'm hoping he tips the pitcher!

Then the announcer's voice came on: "The rules state that only a home player can win the jackpot, but as a consolation prize, we're awarding fifty free Frostys to the West Michigan Whitecaps." I was at an all-time low after pitching that grand slam ball, but that batter might have been even lower. He was a millionaire for five minutes but walked away with nothing but an armful of Frostys.

Somehow I got out of that miserable inning. I went straight to the shower. As I got dressed and walked out to meet Brooke, I was pretty resolved. I'd had an awesome run. I'd earned a scholarship to Georgia Tech, gotten drafted as a junior against all odds, and played professional baseball. I'd been lucky and it was time to move on.

That night, I told Brooke I was going to retire.

She wasn't having it. "You've worked your whole life to get here," she said. "Why on *earth* would you quit? You have the rest of your life to make money. Go chase your dream until someone makes you give it up."

Something happened that night. It became a real pivot point for me. I'd hit rock bottom and decided that wasn't a good place to be—it certainly wasn't where I wanted to be—so I changed course.

After that night, I'm not sure how many innings I went without giving up a run, but it was a lot. That season, which started in such a demoralizing fashion, became one of my better years as a pitcher.

In 2021, it felt a lot like the Democrats were the ones who hit the grand slam.

The GOP let them load up the bases and then threw a pitch they hit out of the park. As a Republican, I felt as low as I had standing on that Kane County field years ago while the Whitecap's slugger triumphantly circled the bases. My party had lost the Big Three, my red state had flipped blue, and my party seemed intent on barreling down a road to irrelevance.

It became crystal clear to me that *this* was our party's pivot point.

★ ★ ★

In 2011, I was a ballplayer-turned-businessman. I'd help run four companies and sold one. I loved the private sector.

Government laws and regulations affected my ventures to varying degrees, and I appreciated the Republican Party's approach to business. But my political interest ended there.

Then I heard a particular Sunday sermon from our pastor. His general message was, "Stop complaining and start getting involved." It struck home because I admitted to myself I'd been doing a lot of complaining recently. Brooke would have agreed. The pastor encouraged us to engage in our communities, maybe even run for office, but most importantly: *Do* something.

Unfortunately for Brooke, I was the guy who took him literally. We walked out of church and I said, "I'm going to run for office." I still remember the surprised look on her face.

I won my first election, the 2012 Republican primary for State House District 26. I scraped by with a 55-vote margin against a longtime representative whose cronies had basically redrawn this district just for him. I was the underdog and interloper. Still, I managed to pull out the primary win—and take the general election in November.

An advantage to being a state representative is you can't give up your day job. I spent three months each year immersed in activity under Georgia's Gold Dome, as our capitol building is called, owing to the Dahlonega, Georgia, gold that coats the dome. The other nine months I remained the businessman I'd been since leaving baseball. I thrived in my roles at the capitol, in business, and at home, and I aimed for another term.

I won reelection in 2014 and in 2016, voters elected me to a third term.

Those same 2016 voters also elected an outsider as president of the United States. And without that precedent, there would be no Lieutenant Governor Geoff Duncan.

I figured that if an outsider businessman could win the White House, maybe this outsider could find a better platform to help people in Georgia and, in particular, help fix our rural healthcare crisis, which had become a priority for me. I resigned my State House seat in September 2017 and gave everything I had to a run for lieutenant governor.

Did I mention it was a longshot run? And I mean a *real* longshot.

I wasn't next in line to run for lieutenant governor. Heck, I wasn't even 50th or 100th in line. The political establishment barely knew my name.

I had a message that mattered to me, however, and it seemed to resonate with voters too: *Policy over politics.*

It means what you think. I'm a policy nerd. I find a problem and want to fix it. I'll look for the best ideas and don't really care which think tank, organization, company, or politician has them. The policy is most important to me because that's what's most important to people. And that mindset allows us to bring together surprising coalitions to help Georgians. I spent nearly two years traveling the state, campaigning hard and sharing that message. A few months before the primary election, my name recognition numbers were still in the basement.

I asked myself what I was doing. Was anyone listening? Did anyone remember who I was or what I said after I walked off a stage? I came back to something a friend had told me. He'd said, "Geoff, you may not be the right guy for this office. You may get ten votes. But if you make this about the journey and not the trophy, you'll win either way. If you share your vision and hopes every time you walk into a room, you'll win."

That kept me going. I made sure my family knew running for office was a journey to help others, not a way to claim a trophy. Helping others meant placing policy over politics to make progress for people.

If there *were* a trophy, that ideal was it.

★ ★ ★

Still today, I'm fine with losing if I'm getting to share what's important to me and what I think is important to Georgia. That's why I didn't shy from stating the truth about our free and fair 2020 election, and that's why I'm sharing some hard truths concerning the GOP's future.

Do you know how many people advised me not to take such strong positions against election fraud?

Do you know how many people told me not to step out of line with the president?

On May 22, 2018, I awaited the results of my first campaign for statewide office. I soon learned that I finished second in a three-way Republican primary for lieutenant governor. The establishment candidate received 48.9 percent, I tallied 26.6 percent, and third place got 24.5 percent.

I had stunned the party. I even surprised myself. I like to think the outcome didn't surprise those who voted for me.

At any length, we forced a runoff, where I faced the candidate backed by the party machine, David Shafer, who'd corralled 48.9 percent of the primary vote. He felt entitled to the office after his 30-year career in professional politics. He was next in line—at least according to the rules made by long-time politicians.

Thankfully, the majority of Georgia Republicans didn't care about the party's rules. I closed the gap in nine weeks and squeaked out 50.14 percent of the vote in the runoff. I won the nomination by 1,597 votes. Georgia Republicans chose me to represent them for lieutenant governor in the November 2018 general election, where I received nearly 2 million votes and won the race.

I'm still humbled by the trust Georgia voters placed in me. I remain grateful and still pinch myself on occasion to make sure this is real.

Did our campaign really go from having less than 2 percent of Georgians know my name in January 2018 to winning 51.6 percent of the statewide vote in the November general election? We really did.

When I stepped into my new role as president of the Georgia senate, I made it clear that the currency I trade is honesty. Senators learned that quickly. If they wanted my help, they needed to be honest. We could work around policy differences and personality differences, but we could not work around lies, half-truths, or omissions. It became a bipartisan policy and I applied it as fairly as I could—and I think I did a good job. I hope senators would tell you the same. I also think they like knowing the president of the senate plays it fair both ways, and when they get mad at me, it's usually because I won't bend the rules or grant a special favor for them. On most of those occasions, they know they shouldn't be asking anyway. The bipartisan honesty policy makes it easy for me too; I only have to follow one set of rules for everyone—not one for my caucus and one for Democrats.

Honesty just means a lot to me. Most Americans feel the same way. They want honesty in their business and in their marriage. They certainly expect it from their children. At heart, I know they want honesty in our politics too. Republicans should be known for that; that should be our brand. We tell the truth and do the right thing. We accept facts and assess them with integrity.

Granted we're a political party, so there's going to be some spin, but I want people to remember my party and me less for what we accomplished and more for how we accomplished it.

In the Georgia Senate and in the Duncan household, if we do right and lose, that's better than doing wrong and winning.

Thinking back to baseball, that's why I didn't use steroids. In late 1990s pro ball, it seemed like more people used steroids than not, but I didn't once seriously think about using them. I couldn't imagine waking up in the Big Leagues and knowing I wasn't there honestly.

And I was *so* close. *Achingly* close. I was one pitch away from the Big Leagues.

Not only were the Big Leagues "big time," but playing just a single game in the majors would basically secure you a lifetime card to coach or manage. There I was, stuck in AAA purgatory for what seemed like forever. A few cycles of anabolic steroids would have given me the edge I needed to throw a bit harder—and that "bit" would have bumped me up.

Brooke and I talked about this together, and we both agreed it wasn't worth it. I never wavered—even though cheating might have meant taking the Marlins' chartered jet instead of riding the bus.

Making the choice not to use steroids even more difficult was the unfortunate fact that my most demoralizing losses seemed to be the games before the longest bus trips. I'd lose a game, then wallow in the loss for the next twelve hours, as the bus rolled along the interstate and *Journey's Greatest Hits* played through my headset. I still have that CD.

I laugh at how appropriate "Don't Stop Believin'" has been for my life.

★ ★ ★

Like every ballplayer, I lost a lot of games during the long journey from Little League. I never liked to lose. I never got used to it. I also saw a lot of other guys lose. Some quietly walked to the shower, some kicked the furniture all the way to the locker room. They'd tell you they never got used to it either. Most of us did figure out how to level with ourselves and learn from the losses. We had to—we knew we had to play again the next day and do better. Like so many other people, I've found my best and most valuable lessons in my toughest losses.

When Congress convened on January 6, 2021, few Republicans had fully acknowledged the president's loss. We witnessed the tragic culmination of their actions on live television. Even after Joe Biden's January 20 inauguration, around three out of four Republicans *still* didn't accept our new president had won fair and square.

Here's my question: How does a political party learn from a loss if it doesn't think it lost?

The early answer seems to be: It doesn't.

I found responses from Republican Party chairs worrisome, especially given our candidate lost by 7 million popular votes and 74 electoral votes. In 2016, the president called that exact electoral margin "a landslide." In 2020, it thrilled me to see the GOP find down-ballot success, especially on local levels where candidates ran on tangible results and conservative policies. Tactically speaking however, Republicans can't ignore that our top-of-ticket lost on November 3, 2020, and we lost our Senate majority two months later. The party machine didn't seem to care, however.

"As far as I'm concerned, everything is great," said a GOP district chair.

"It wasn't a matter of our candidate, it was a matter of the process," explained a county chair.

"Our president absolutely grew our party," observed a state chair. "I think as Republicans we just need to remain on the course."

And another state chair said, "I don't think there's a post-mortem about losing the election. The real post-mortem is about how do we protect our electoral system."

Months after the election, most national Republican leaders still wouldn't admit the president had lost; you could still see doublethink's grip as GOP leaders never questioned the legitimacy of their *own* election. Some are gradually moving on, while others will never call President Biden's election fair, either because they believe massive fraud occurred or they're too afraid to level with their constituents who they misled after the election.

I'm not sure which is worse.

I'll tell you what's at least equally bad: *blaming everyone but yourself.*

Imagine if every Fortune 500 CEO blamed a bogeyman after every tough quarter: bad weather, unfair competition, government policy, bad middle management, inaccurate data, China, Democrats—you pick. How would business ever improve? It wouldn't. American companies would lose money and fall behind. American industry would lose out to other countries.

Not a single corporate board member or shareholder would tolerate leaders who didn't accept responsibility for company performance. Further, they all expect their companies to create ecosystems that foster continual improvement. They know that's how companies create more value and win more customers. A board wouldn't condemn a leader for a bad quarter, but they'd want her to make a plan to fix the problem systemically. And making an effective plan starts with identifying what went wrong. A leader must admit everything didn't go right so the entire team can do better next time.

It's fascinating to me that investors with millions sunk into companies demand CEOs produce returns on their investments but many of the same investors sunk millions into the president's campaign and aren't demanding anyone learn lessons and fix problems.

If the president and his lieutenants are that unresponsive to their big investors, do we think they'll be any more responsive to the real people in America?

The former president didn't learn a thing. Despite his loss of the White House and Senate, the man who had always celebrated winners and scorned losers found a way to retain his influence and not admit anything went wrong—except "fraud."

He convinced many Republicans to follow along. During his second impeachment trial, an *Economist* poll put his support among Republicans at 88 percent. The February 13, 2021, vote on impeachment emphasized many Republicans still valued his grace above all else. Only seven Republican senators voted to convict him. The others used verbal and constitutional gymnastics to dodge the question, avoid taking action, or avoid laying blame on the president.

These collective actions damaged our democratic republic and the Republican Party. They tarnished our brand and place in history. They also signal nobody needs to be concerned that our candidate lost by 7 million popular votes and 74 electoral votes.

"No lessons here, folks. Let's put our heads back into the ground."

All of this just left me shaking my head.

Part of this perception problem may come from the media's visuals. Seeing a big county-by-county electoral map of the United States makes a Republican feel good. Red districts seem to blanket the country, effectively covering up the demographic and political trends threatening the party. Those maps present a false reality because, of course, land mass won doesn't equate to either victory or consensus. That familiar red-and-blue, state-by-state map builds a false overconfidence in our platforms. It helps stoke the disbelief and outrage we saw after the 2020 election: "How could our candidate possibly lose when most of the country is beet red?"

I'm a Republican so I like seeing red states and counties as much as anyone, but people not acres cast ballots. After the 2020 election, numerous outlets printed maps that showed geographic results adjusted for real impact on the electoral vote. Our great swaths of red get much smaller and the mass of blue grows considerably. Geographically-large red states like Montana suddenly become 25 percent the size of small blue states like Massachusetts. Electoral maps like these certainly help me think more carefully about our party's direction and strategy.

The popular vote also indicates where America is heading. Sure, swings of 10,000 to 150,000 votes in several states could have flipped the Electoral College in 2020, and sure, the state of California has an outsized influence on the popular vote. But while I support the Founders' original system for presidential elections, I don't want to cling to the Electoral College as our only means of victory down the road—especially when battleground states where the GOP can win today are trending blue or purple. Here's the alarm bell: The Republican Party has won the popular vote one time—once—since 1988.

Democrat Bill Clinton bested George H. W. Bush by 5.8 million votes in 1992 and beat Bob Dole by 8.2 million in 1996. Republican George W. Bush won the Electoral College vote in 2000 but lost the popular vote by 543,000 to Al Gore. Bush then became the last Republican to win the popular vote when he beat John Kerry by 3 million in the next cycle. In 2008, Barack Obama beat John McCain by 9.5 million and then defeated Mitt Romney by 4.9 million. Hillary Clinton won the popular vote by 2.8 million in 2016 and Joe Biden won it by 7 million in 2020.

It's hard to claim mandates when a majority of voters cast ballots against your policies.

Any coach worth their salt would study results from losses like these, especially since the former president left office with a dismal approval rating of 34 percent. My coaches would have called in the team to discuss what went wrong and how we could improve. Then we'd take what we learned and move on to the next game.

The Republican Party leadership isn't calling anyone into the locker room. Nobody is discussing what went wrong, because everyone pretends *nothing* went wrong in the election—except rampant fraud.

Clearly *something* went wrong afterwards on January 6. And those issues aren't disappearing just because there's a new man at 1600 Pennsylvania Avenue.

Denialism, misinformation, and misplaced blame will not put a Republican back in the White House in 2024. What will? Honestly studying our losses, addressing our internal splits, and offering a way forward that captures more voters from more places. Let's talk straight about what went wrong and what comes next for the Grand Old Party after losing the Big Three: the U.S. House, Senate, and White House. How can we find common ground and common purpose among our own factions? What can the 2020 election teach us?

The 2020 elections offer three particularly important lessons to Republicans.

1. Our tent must expand.
2. Our tent *can* expand.
3. The sideshows have to stop.

1. OUR TENT MUST EXPAND

Democrats and Republicans alike face the challenge of balancing committed, activist party leaders with the less-committed non-activists who comprise much of the grassroots membership. Those active in state and local party machinery often take stronger positions than party members as a whole. Moderates just don't get as fired up or involved, especially when getting involved means wading into a divisive environment with which they're just not comfortable. Nowadays, many Republicans or former Republicans feel ostracized for not agreeing with every plank of the party platform.

I'll note that in 2020, the GOP had no policy platform. Its platform was literally whatever the president said it was at a particular moment. In theory someone could be on the outs one week and back in the next if the president simply changed his mind.

I call these alienated Republicans and other middle-of-the-road folks the "silenced majority," and I've always taken comfort knowing they're there.

They became a great comfort for me in those hard weeks following the 2020 election. After I'd come off camera, having given yet another interview where I called out the Fraud Hoax, I'd walk to the car and scroll through my Twitter feed. I'd find messages from all fifty states, from Republicans and independents, conservatives and moderates, encouraging me to keep speaking the truth.

I think these folks still appreciate what "conservative" means. They know what "Republican" ought to mean. During my entire two-year campaign for lieutenant governor, the only thing attacked about my voting record was that it was too conservative. I'm a serious conservative who believes in limited government and the rule of law, states' rights, and personal responsibility. I believe in ensuring the safety and security of all Americans. You may be able to attack me politically, but you'd be hard-pressed to attack me for not being conservative.

My gut tells me that conservatives have quit the GOP in droves over the past four years. To me, the consistently high percentage of Republicans supporting the former president indicate that those who don't support him have left. Identifying as Republican and supporting the former president have almost become interchangeable. Being conservative is less and less a defining characteristic of a Republican. Instead, blind loyalty and subservience to the former president has become the standard.

I am still hopeful, however. Cracks keep emerging in the party monolith built by the former president. A Gallup poll released in February 2021 showed that among self-identified Republicans, support for the Republican Party dropped 12 percent from November 2020 to February 2021, landing at 78 percent. That's still an extraordinarily high percentage for a group of people who theoretically don't like centralized authority, but there is daylight between Republicans and the party where there wasn't before.

Among all respondents, the GOP's favorability dropped 6 percent to 37 percent. In early 2021, just 27 percent of independents approved of the president—and this is where I believe we see former Republicans. They're embarrassed to be Republicans and they don't approve of the last four years. The president's approval among those people who'd *voted* for him in November had plummeted a full 22 percent to reach 62 percent.

That doesn't set off alarms?

Disenchanted conservatives and political moderates are vital for a winning Republican coalition. As the GOP loses them, the party drifts closer to permanent minority status. Now, you may tell me to look at states led by Republican legislatures or governors or to look at the GOP gains in the U.S. House.

I'd respectfully ask you to look ten years down the road.

Shortly after President Biden entered the White House, the Arizona Republican Party doubled down on not learning lessons from 2020. Since 1952, every Republican candidate for president has carried Arizona, except one. In 2020, a coalition of Arizona Democrats, independents, and alienated Republicans elected Joe Biden and ousted a sitting Republican U.S. Senator. Arizona flipped blue.

On January 23, the Arizona Republican Party needlessly censured two Republicans who'd supported Joe Biden: former Senator Jeff Flake and Senator John McCain's widow, Cindy. They also censured the state's Republican governor, who'd supported the president but ultimately certified the state's vote for Joe Biden.

Doug Ducey stood up to lots of pressure and, like we did in Georgia, refused to call a special session of the legislature so the Republican majority could overturn the results of Arizona's free and fair election.

Good for you, Governor Ducey.

The first weeks of 2021 saw more than 9,000 Arizona voters leave the Republican Party to register as independents, Libertarians, or Democrats. The party was doing its best to run out anyone not in lock step with the president—and they were digging a hole in the process. In a state that is now clearly purple, a party that just lost two statewide races seemed to be excluding voters instead of growing its ranks. And they'll never rev up their remaining base more than they did in 2020 so please tell me how this makes electoral sense.

Parties in other states drew the same hard line. The North Carolina GOP censured its senior U.S. senator, as did the Louisiana GOP. State parties in Georgia, Maine, Nebraska, Ohio, Pennsylvania, and other states all considered censuring or did censure Republicans for not supporting the president sufficiently in various ways, including impeachment votes. "My party, right or wrong?"

The president's margin of victory or loss was 0.3 percent in Arizona, 0.26 percent in Georgia, 1.3 percent in North Carolina, and 1.18 percent in Pennsylvania. Especially in these states, why are state party leaders chasing out everyone who doesn't support the president come hell or high water?

Their states are purple. They can't afford to lose Republicans.

But they are. Twelve thousand Republicans left the party in Pennsylvania in the weeks immediately following January 6. One-third of them lived in critical suburban counties around Philadelphia. Eight thousand left the party in North Carolina during the same time. In the week after the riots, the California GOP lost 33,000 members. In Colorado, 4,600 Republicans quit the party in one week. By end of business on January 8, two counties surrounding Miami, Florida, saw 1,000 voters un-register as Republicans. Three counties around Tampa saw 2,000 leave the GOP.

Those figures come from the week or weeks immediately following January 6. The trend will likely continue if the party doubles down on its current course. That will lead to more defections in places the party cannot afford to lose voters. The battleground states of Arizona, Florida, Georgia, North Carolina, and Pennsylvania hold 91 combined electoral votes. If Republicans continue de-registering at these rates, that's the ballgame.

Elements of the Republican Party in Georgia took a cue from Arizona and made plans to censure the governor, secretary of state, and me for not supporting the president. Someone slipped me a "Censure Lt. Governor Geoff Duncan" template, one of several that were sent to Republicans around the state. Here's the text:

WHEREAS, it has been brought to the collective attention of the (your local GOP) Lt. Gov. Geoff Duncan stood by and did nothing to help President Donald Trump and Georgia Republicans in their fight against election fraud and in fact, ridiculed the claims of election fraud; and WHEREAS, Lt. Governor Duncan denied there was election fraud and frequently appeared on leftist media outlets, including television interviews, and strongly attacked Pres. Trump and Georgia Republicans that believed there was election fraud. Duncan even told CNN's Jake Tapper that he was disgusted by President Trump's claims of election fraud; and WHEREAS, Lt. Governor Duncan retaliated against Georgia Senators that spoke out about the rampant election fraud and held hearings to educate Georgians about the fraud. Duncan removed them as Chairmen of Senate Committees; and NOW, THEREFORE, BE IT RESOLVED BY THE (your local GOP) that the delegates of this convention do hereby censure Lt. Governor Geoff Duncan and urge him not to seek re-election in 2022.

Okay, I didn't help the president and his followers fight election fraud because there was no election fraud to fight. And anyone who knows me understands I don't ridicule people. If asking politicians to stop fanning the flames of anger with mountains of misinformation counts as ridicule, however, I'm guilty. I *will* call balls and strikes. The "leftist media outlets" with which I spoke included Fox News, PBS, and the BBC. The public largely respects the journalistic integrity of the latter two. Fox was considered conservative until it (correctly) called Arizona for Joe Biden. Like me, Fox News also landed in hot water for telling the truth.

Yes, I was "disgusted" by the president's claims because they were dangerous and untrue—I still feel the same.

I knew those claims might lead to something exactly like the January 6 riot, which desecrated our Capitol and resulted in *seven* deaths and hundreds of the president's followers being arrested and having their lives ruined. Too bad for them that real juries will be trying their cases, not the U.S. Senate.

Nobody in their right mind would condone their actions—I emphatically do not.

Clearly and sadly, the falsehoods selfishly spread by our party leaders, for their own political and financial gain, took advantage of these citizens' emotions and stirred those emotions to a boiling point they would never have reached had the president graciously conceded the election in November.

I did remove several Republican leaders from their committee chairmanships partially for their roles in aggressively spreading untrue and debunked fraud claims, giving Rudy Giuliani a platform to spread his outlandish lies, and for engaging in conversations with the president about overriding Georgia's constitution to overturn the election. I wasn't retaliating; I'm not petty. These senators had lost the trust of fellow senators and they had lost the trust of the president of the senate (me). I was convinced beyond the shadow of a doubt that it wasn't just my opinion that they lacked the credibility to carry out their duties as chairmen.

I just don't tolerate behavior like they displayed—not anywhere and not from anyone, and especially not from members of the Georgia Senate.

I promise you if the GOP rejects folks who tell the truth, especially great honest leaders such as Georgia's governor and secretary of state, the party will not win another statewide election in Georgia anytime in the near future. Our state's demographics will continue to shift and make Georgia increasingly purple. If our party doubles down on rancor and purity, it will continue to lose registered voters, just as Democrats are registering more and more. The party won't win statewide and soon won't be able to win competitive legislative districts either.

It seems the GOP wants to make a point, not a difference. It's madness.

Nationally, what does it say when the former president and the Republican Party attack successful and respected conservatives such as George W. Bush?

Such as Mitch McConnell, the man most responsible for the president's slew of conservative judicial appointments?

Such as long-serving Republican Senator Pat Toomey, who the president falsely insinuated had been complicit in "massive" election fraud?

Such as the respected Republican woman and conservative House leader Liz Cheney, who faced a shameful all-out assault from House Republicans and was ousted from her leadership role for holding the president to account yet never backed down and instead showed the courage our leaders genuinely need? She'll now face primary opposition from the right.

Such as Senator Ben Sasse, a dedicated conservative who in 2020 received more votes than any candidate in Nebraska history while noticeably outperforming the president?

It says we're not serious about putting principle before party. We're not serious about winning big elections. We're not serious about making a difference. The GOP cannot win at state and national levels long-term if it doesn't welcome conservative leaders like these into its tent. Nor can it win if it doesn't welcome conservatives and moderates who don't subscribe to every element of the president's platform and who don't hold him above the law.

The GOP has a choice: Stop following this crazy path to nowhere or get used to losing.

If our own divisive and dysfunctional politics aren't enough to convince leaders our party needs a better path, here's a flurry of other dangerous trends. Leaders can discount them as "fake news" or "biased," if they wish. Or Republican leaders can acknowledge these very real trends and adjust.

Women are the largest single voting block in the American system. A pre-election poll showed Joe Biden leading the president by 23 percent among women. The actual election results were more similar to 2016's 13-point gender gap, however. Women broke for Biden and other Democrats by around 15 percent. That's a gap we can close, but it's a killer if we don't.

More than 16 million Latinos voted in 2020, a 31 percent increase from 2016. And while the GOP made some very positive inroads, Latinos voted blue in overwhelming numbers. A UCLA study of thirteen key states (including battlegrounds Georgia, Arizona, Florida, Pennsylvania, Texas, and Wisconsin) found Latinos voted for Biden by 3-to-1 margins in 9 states. Biden's margin was less than 2-to-1 in only one state: Florida. It's no wonder. More than half of Latinos (51 percent) felt the GOP was "hostile" toward them, according to a 2019 study.

Some people think Latinos are the country's fastest-growing ethnic group. They're not; Asians are. Asian Americans often have higher incomes and own businesses too. They have a great

GOP profile, and in 1992, they voted Republican 2 to 1. In 2020, however, they went Democratic 2 to 1, with 63 percent voting for Biden and 31 percent for the president.

The GOP cannot allow this shift to continue. We must address the concerns of these Americans, welcome them, and make a better case for our policies. If we don't do that, it will only add to our troubles.

Harvard Kennedy School professor Thomas Patterson looked at current voting patterns by demographic groups. Then he projected what the 2032 election might look like if those groups continue voting the same way: Shifting demographics would give Democrats a 59 percent to 41 percent advantage over Republicans in 2032 based solely on population changes. The groups I've discussed are growing faster than the traditional white Republican base, which is shrinking in many places. Without white evangelicals, the GOP would have earned less than 40 percent of the national vote in 2020. It's worth noting that white evangelicals were 25 percent of the population in the 1990s. Now they're just one-sixth.

If we cannot grow our tent and welcome women and these growing ethnic groups, the GOP will have a bleak future.

But I have good news! A better path forward exists if we're just wise enough to take it.

Read on.

2. OUR TENT *CAN* EXPAND

Independents went for Biden 54 percent to 41 percent in 2020. That's not an insurmountable gap. With the right messages, policies, and tone, we can win back this critical block.

Consider the former president's after-office approval among independents however. Only 32 percent of them view the

GOP favorably. A full 50 percent of independents thought the president should resign after the Capitol riots and his approval rating among independents was 34 percent. The numbers may change, but in 2021, it sure looks like Republicans running in the image of the former president shouldn't expect much help from the vital center.

Here's a secret: The vital center is larger than ever.

In February 2021, for the first time in Gallup's ongoing party affiliation survey, 50 percent of respondents identified as independent. And that growth didn't just come from GOP losses. Before the 2020 election, 31 percent identified as Republican and 31 percent identified as Democratic. Both parties chased away 6 percent of their voters in two months. At President Biden's inauguration, 25 percent of Americans identified Republican and 25 percent identified as Democratic. We know that it's more important than ever to win independent votes, and we know that being a monolithic party isn't how to do it. We will not win long-term nationally without at least 50 percent of the independent vote.

We'd better go get it.

I firmly believe a more inclusive candidate with a better message can reach independents and even some Democrats fed up with their party's own issues and leftward lurches. The "Reasoned Republican" candidates I envision can bring these swing voters back into the GOP's camp.

We can't gerrymander our way to victory in statewide and presidential elections. We must move our feet and share a better message.

We shouldn't miss that candidates can carry a compelling economic message when they talk about growth in inclusive terms. Joe Biden talked about economic policies such as a higher minimum wage that directly affected pocketbooks of workers. Too often, the GOP talks more about policies that directly affect corporations and business owners, but not about those that directly affect workers.

The old trickle-down argument is a weak one. Joe Biden's message and tone ultimately didn't win him Florida, but he *did* help influence a significant majority of Floridians—61 percent—to vote to increase the minimum wage to $15 over time, even as they reelected the president by more than three points and more than 400,000 votes.

The 2020 election had notably positive down ballot results for the GOP: The party proved itself able to flip seats and engage moderates. Republicans won back a dozen seats in the U.S. House of Representatives. The number of Republican women in the GOP House delegation nearly tripled, jumping from 13 in 2019 to 30 in 2021. That's still less than 15 percent of our Congressional caucus, so work remains but that big increase shows our ability to change and grow our coalition. In the state of California, where Democrats control the legislature and governor's office, the GOP flipped four congressional seats.

The party made inroads into communities of color too. Democrats lost eight congressional districts where Joe Biden won. Six were majority people of color. Voters in these districts voted against the president but for Republican representatives. In fact, progressive champions like Alexandria Ocasio-Cortez, Ilhan Omar, and Rashida Tlaib underperformed Joe Biden in their districts.

The former president's claim that he "won the largest share of non-white voters of any Republican in 60 years" wasn't true (just look back to George W. Bush in 2004). But the 2020 election did give us proof that we can make inroads into these growing communities.

An encouraging anecdote comes from California, where a majority of voters are Latino, Black, or Asian. The state's voters rejected Proposition 16, which would have repealed a ban on affirmative action. More than 57 percent of voters opposed the measure: They didn't want affirmative action in their state.

Non-white populations are neither monolithic nor necessarily against conservative ideas.

We saw that the GOP can, in fact, expand its tent. The president received more support from Asian, Black, and Hispanic voters than he did in 2016, even with all his sideshows. He gained seven points among Asians. Look at Miami-Dade County where 75 percent of precincts are majority Hispanic. The president won 53.5 percent of the vote in those precincts— versus just 40 percent in 2016. That translated to him winning 61 percent of the precincts in 2020 versus 26 percent of them in 2016. Republicans' pro-business, pro-life, and pro-freedom approaches resonated even though the president's rhetoric and stance on immigration alienated many in the Latino community. He made inroads and the GOP won Florida.

In Houston, Texas, nearly 90 percent of the surrounding county's majority-Hispanic precincts shifted toward the president, which defied pollsters and helped deliver Texas to the president by a healthy margin of 6 percent. In heavily Latino southwest Texas, Democratic margins shrunk considerably. In Zapata County with its 93 percent Hispanic population, the president gained 36 points from 2016 to 2020; he lost by 33 percent in 2016 and won by 6 percent in 2020. In Hidalgo County, he gained 23 percent from 2016. Moving west, in Arizona's Maricopa County, the president made gains in 61 percent of majority-Hispanic precincts, but the shift wasn't enough to win the state.

The president earned 32 percent of the Hispanic vote overall in 2020, a 3 percent increase from 2016. That starts to push the GOP back toward the levels of support received by George W. Bush (35 percent and 44 percent in 2000 and 2004). As Latino voters become more established, I think they find many of our positions more compelling as they're trying to grow their businesses, work hard, be self-sufficient, and live out their faith.

We also need to realize different Latino communities have had different experiences. We must take time to get to know them—truly *empathize* with them—so we can know how best to help them achieve their aspirations.

Many have citizenship that traces back generations and run prosperous companies. Some have close ties to new immigrants from Mexico and Latin America. Others had their worldview shaped by regimes in countries like Cuba and Venezuela.

The lessons here are that our pro-business, pro-life, pro-freedom messages resonate among these groups. Remember George W. Bush won 49 percnt of the Latino vote as governor of Texas.

Let's not ignore Latinos because outreach isn't easy, or we don't understand them well (yet).

Let's not lose them with needlessly inflammatory language around immigration. Let's not make their hill harder to climb by cutting programs and making healthcare more expensive and inaccessible. We knew this a decade ago, if not more. Even though the GOP's 2012 post-election autopsy pointed to the necessity of engaging Latino communities, the party has fallen short on doing the real work and we have paid the price.

The president's share of the Black vote lagged behind Presidents Nixon, Ford, and Reagan's shares, but he did gain 4 percent from 2020, reaching 12 percent. He did this despite four years of divisive language, flirtations with white supremacy, and poor handling of racial justice protests.

What if he had showed understanding and empathy?

What if he'd responded to the needs and conditions that fueled the protests?

What if he didn't intentionally stoke the very fires Blacks felt were burning up their freedom?

Republicans are the freedom party! We should stand up for freedom and opportunity for everyone. Here, we failed, yet it seems some daylight remains.

Another observation: American elections are becoming more predictable. Winners rarely overperform or underperform what you'd expect given the demographics of their constituency. If a state or congressional district is likely to give 55 percent to Republicans, that's what they'll do and it doesn't matter who the candidate is. Candidates seem to matter less, and party matters more. But it's useful to look at the handful of cases where candidates outperform – where they do better than demographics would predict.

One example is Adam Kinzinger, a Republican member of Congress from Illinois who has adopted a decidedly reasoned tone. He overperformed expectations in his district by 5 points showing how some moderation and bridge-building can lead to electoral success. He didn't let tone and sideshows obscure his conservative message and he won with support from independents and moderates.

His reward? In January 2021, his district's party leadership took steps to censure him for his vote to impeach the president for inciting the January 6 riot. They're recruiting someone to challenge him in the 2022 primary. If the challenger wins, the party is almost certainly replacing a Republican who can build a winning coalition with one who can't.

The local party's leaders will have sent a message to Adam, but they will undoubtedly have sent a Democrat to Washington.

Do we want to make a point or make a difference?

3. THE SIDESHOWS NEED TO STOP

The president's loss seemed like a death from thousands of little cuts.

The third counting of Georgia ballots showed a final margin of 11,779 votes. That's 11,779 votes out of more than 5 million cast, a 0.24 percent margin. Did the president *lose* 11,779 votes with his tone and unnecessary forays into the fringe?

I think so.

Starting with Georgia, what if he'd not attacked our Republican governor, who citizens believed was navigating the pandemic relatively well?

What if he'd not attacked civil rights icon and Georgia Congressman John Lewis after this national hero died in July 2020?

If he'd gotten as many votes as our state's GOP congressional candidates, he would have won Georgia by 16,000 votes.

Looking beyond Georgia, what if he'd just put on a more presidential performance in the first 2020 debate?

What if he'd not attacked Arizona's beloved senator and war hero John McCain?

What if he hadn't alienated Senator McCain's widow? Would he have kept 10,457 votes, which were his margin of loss in the Grand Canyon State? You can make a strong argument for "Yes."

What if he'd clearly condemned white supremacy?

What if on March 1, 2020, he'd told his followers to start wearing masks—even red Make America Great Again masks—and showed leadership, compassion, and intellectual honesty during the pandemic?

What if he'd not tried to involve the Ukraine in domestic politics and thus avoided his first impeachment?

What if he'd paid more respect to the truth?

What if he'd stopped the name-calling?

What if he put down his phone?

If he'd taken just some of these actions, I'm convinced he would have kept 12,000 votes and won Georgia.

I can't speak for other close states, but my hunch is he could have prevailed there, too, with a little more civility and message discipline.

And we're just talking about not *losing* votes.

Can you imagine the votes he could have gained if he'd also dug into his policy wins and focused on those instead of enemies and grievances? Remember when I suggested he talk about how his policies were helping Georgians and he instead vented about CNN? That was one of countless chances for him to win—or at least, not lose—votes. He and his allies passed on those opportunities again and again. The sideshows won. And the sideshows and misinformation haven't stopped since the election.

Fellow Republicans, let me say this: Falsehood undermines freedom.

Falsehood kills America's freedom-centric party electorally, as a community, and as a conservative movement. It also sows distrust, which then drives the party machine and government to create more rules and regulations. It undermines the community bonds that encourage neighbors to help neighbors and solve local problems without looking to the government.

I promise you government will step into the void and slowly siphon our precious freedoms. Dishonesty also undermines trust in our democratic republic and the institutions and systems that support it.

As Republicans, we don't think government has every answer. We respect its vital, albeit limited, role. If its institutions collapse or cease to function, we are in deep, deep trouble. Some may say that's exactly what we need to happen, and I could not disagree more. It unleashes rule by the strongest and the loudest. If elections and political bodies no longer hold the People's trust, every decision and every election could boil down to who yells the loudest and who holds the most power.

As a party, we need to stop tolerating the volume of misinformation produced and spread by our right wing. A group of researchers at NYU analyzed social media content and found far-right content garnered far more engagement from users or followers—400 to 800 percent more—than right, center, left, or far-left content. And engagement around far-right misinformation was nearly double the engagement around accurate information posted by far-right groups. This all means people in the party's right wing are reposting, discussing, and sharing misinformation at astounding and alarming volumes compared to other slices of the political spectrum. Even the villains of the far left interact with more than twice as much accurate content as they do misinformation. We conservatives are allowing ourselves to be poisoned by misinformation. Our grip on reality—and our credibility with key voters such as independents, moderates, and even many conservatives—will continue to slip if we don't take a stand and stop this nonsense.

Remember, Georgia is an example of how falsehood undermines not only the country, but the party and conservative cause. Angry Republicans knowingly gave life to the Fraud Hoax after the November 3 election. They convinced some three-quarters of the party that rampant fraud flipped the election. They said our election system couldn't be trusted. Well, Republicans listened. When the January 5 U.S. Senate runoff arrived, an estimated 400,000-plus Republicans who voted in November stayed home. Our antics so motivated the opposition that 225,000 people who *didn't* vote in November *did* vote in January; a significant portion of them represented typically Democratic demographics. Georgia's two Senate seats flipped blue giving the Democrats control of the U.S. Senate.

If the GOP keeps up false narratives, future elections in Georgia and elsewhere will see Republicans not voting or voting against party candidates who they realize are spreading misinformation and fear instead of solving real problems.

For a highly consequential example of choosing sideshows over leadership, just look at how the former president handled the pandemic. We learned in Bob Woodward's infamous interview that the president clearly knew the facts about the coronavirus but chose to politicize this global threat to boost his image and agenda—and divide Americans with the one issue that should have united us. And many party members went right along with him.

As a direct result, instead of leading the world in an effective response to the pandemic, the United States led the world in COVID-19 cases and related deaths. The then-president overruled scientists, gave false information, and failed to provide wise guidance to states or just about anyone else for that matter.

One of the president's greatest regrets from 2020 could be that by politicizing and thus bumbling the pandemic, he may have cost himself reelection. Most other Americans' greatest regret is likely the more than 500,000 lives we lost.

These Republican sideshows have real consequences, and they have to stop.

★ ★ ★

Here's some good news for Republicans: America remains a center-right nation.

In January 2021, Gallup reported that 36 percent of Americans identified as conservative and 35 percent identified as moderate. Only 25 percent identified as liberal. Conservatives lost a point during 2020, but these numbers still encourage me, and I believe we can increase our conservative numbers with good policy and tone and engage more moderates the same way. The conservative message resonates, but our party's more recent tone does not.

What I know for sure is that if we only play to hard conservatives, we won't continue winning elections outside of gerrymandered districts.

In my Peach State, 53.7 percent of voters cast a ballot for a Republican state senator. Across the country the GOP holds 27 governorships and leads 31 state legislatures. We gained one more chamber and one more governorship in the 2020 election; we won 8 of 11 gubernatorial races. In 22 states, voters gave Republicans control of their legislative *and* executive branches. The 2020 election saw Republicans gain 12 seats in the U.S. House of Representatives. In the U.S. Senate, the GOP reclaimed an Alabama seat but dropped seats in Arizona,

Colorado, and Georgia. I'm convinced we could have saved Georgia's two seats had the party not fixated on the election-fraud storyline.

Look at New Hampshire: The Granite State voted for Joe Biden and reelected two Democratic U.S. representatives and one Democratic U.S. senator. But it overwhelmingly elected local Republicans. Voters reelected a Republican governor and they flipped control of the state's senate and house from Democratic to Republican.

I believe citizens recognize the value of conservative policies, particularly at the local and state level. National sideshows and flashpoint issues may push them away, but they know our core policies work for real people in their state. Let's not give them an excuse to vote against us.

Republicans don't need to look any further than my state of Georgia to see how conservative policies improve life for everyone. Unfortunately, instead of capitalizing on these results and building a winning coalition in Georgia, the party humored sideshows and echoed the divisive tactics of national leaders.

Georgia should have been a lock for Republicans. Instead, we lost the presidential vote and both Senate seats. Nobody took them from us; we *lost* them.

Sometimes you do only have yourself to blame.

Let's stick to good policy and governing. That's where we can win.

In the end, the 2020 election showed us the electorate appreciates our core principles but not our lack of inclusiveness, harsh tones, distractions, and instability. I hope that gives us grounding and courage—and *faith*—that we can expand our appeal among America's changing electorate. And to those of you who've been silenced or chased out of the party, the GOP needs you back. We can become your party again.

The party of Lincoln, Eisenhower, and Reagan can again be a party for big ideas, different ideas, vibrant debate, civility, and respect.

A party of hope.

A party rooted in history and traditional principles but shaped by modern times and realities.

A party re-committed to securing everyone's God-given freedom to thrive.

To those who see the former president as the party, I welcome a new dialogue. The party will never go back to the past—that's not my vision or yours.

I believe with all my heart that if we commit to accepting one another and agree to move beyond the unhelpful division and diversions of the past four years, we can lead a bigger and more dynamic party toward a better future.

I call this movement GOP 2.0, and it's ultimately a movement powered by something that might surprise you until you really think about it: love.

6

★ ★ ★

FAITH, LOVE, AND POLITICS

WE CANNOT HAVE A CONVERSATION ABOUT THE FUTURE OF OUR nation or party without some grounding in basic American and human principles. The principles of faith have always formed our community's bedrock and our common human touchpoints. The core values of faithful people may be the last thing on which we all agree. I'm not going to share my personal testimony or explain why the Almighty supports this or that agenda. I am talking about how faith—which I've always considered a verb—must be part of Republican politics if we want a future worth having.

These pages aren't about Christianity, although I am an enthusiastic Christian. Like most Americans, I look to faith for strength and guidance in an uncertain yet beautiful world. It grounds me, nurtures our family, and gives me a good lens for viewing life. It does the same for people of most every religion or belief. That's as it should be.

In these pages, I'd like to talk about a teacher named Jesus who lived 2,000 years ago. I'd like to talk about what he did, how he treated people, and how he sparked hope and an enduring movement. Americans are a faith-centered people with many religions among us. Almost all of us do our best to abide by morals and principles of faith in our daily lives. So I'm not going to talk about how we govern ourselves as a society without talking about how we govern ourselves as individuals.

Still, I debated including this in the book. I'm well aware even mentioning the word "Jesus" can trigger an avalanche of reactions and labels. I'm trusting readers will understand my goal, which isn't to preach but rather to hold up the one universal example that I hope might have the strength to bind up our wounds and draw us together. So whatever your background, please bear with me and read on.

As a Christian, I do my best to use Jesus as my lens and bedrock. He is the foundation used by my faith. Research shows most Republicans are Christians, but many readers will follow different religions. Or maybe you were a Christian years ago but aren't anymore. You may be uncertain. You may have no faith or religion at all. But you likely have a similar ethical or spiritual lens for viewing the world, and that lens is formed by values most Americans appreciate.

Today we desperately need everyone to apply their own personal, ethical, spiritual, or religious lens to our national political life.

I haven't seen polling on this topic, but I would almost guarantee that an overwhelming majority of Americans prefer their elected leaders to have some sort of guiding faith. I'd also bet they'd rather see that faith play out through those leaders' actions than hear about it in speeches.

My parents understood the value of raising kids grounded in faith. Our family moved seven times before I was seventeen, so we never had a church home for long. Every time we arrived in a new town, however, my parents found a church congregation where we'd be comfortable. Regardless of the congregation, these churches taught me about a particular Jewish rabbi who turned the tables on religion: Jesus. As a kid, I thought Jesus seemed much more pragmatic and far less cryptic than the God I learned about in the Bible, so I gravitated toward his example.

The coming decades saw me following Jesus's teachings on some occasions and setting them aside on others. My freshman year at Georgia Tech was an example of the latter. Being on the country's top-ranked college baseball team and living in a metropolis like Atlanta became a distraction. School became a third or fourth priority and lackluster grades almost cost me my spot on the team. If I hadn't gotten my act together, I would have missed the once-in-a-lifetime opportunity of the College World Series. Luckily, a familiar angel arrived on campus the next year: my high school girlfriend, Brooke. She helped refocus my priorities for the better.

Years later, Brooke and I were back in Georgia raising our family when I ran into a friend from the Georgia Tech baseball team. It turned out we lived near each other and he invited Brooke and me to church and then to his small group. Those two invitations led my family to dive head-first into faith, which continues to fuel this journey I'm on today.

On my second day in elected office, an invitation to a joint Georgia House–Senate Bible study group landed on my desk. Being a new state representative isn't different from being the new guy in any organization, and I leapt at the chance to meet new colleagues. I woke up early on a cold January day in 2013 and drove forty miles to downtown Atlanta to hear a message from the former governor of a nearby state.

Deep down, I had prepared myself to hear another talk that put Christianity in the middle of politics for all the wrong reasons. But I thought meeting fellow representatives would be worth enduring the political-religious cocktail that tends to paint religion either Red or Blue.

We were finishing our eggs when the speaker walked up to the microphone and said, "Did you know Jesus wasn't a Christian?"

The speaker's question struck me. I'd never considered this fact in quite this way. Sure, I knew Jesus was Jewish, but he ended up being Christian, right? That morning it dawned on me that, no, he didn't end up being a Christian. Nobody even used the term "Christian" until decades after Jesus died—and the people who first said it used it as a derogatory label! People didn't like these disciples of Jesus. They couldn't understand people who would follow this dusty teacher who had no money or pedigree. His followers were a strange mishmash of fishermen, farmers, merchants, laborers, nobles, and homemakers. Unlike followers of other religions or sects of the time, Jesus's followers didn't make blood offerings, they didn't observe class barriers, and they talked about helping other people. None of these early Jesus followers called themselves Christian. Some thought of themselves as "followers of the way." Most simply knew one another as disciples or followers of Jesus, people who thought a young, eccentric guy named Jesus offered a better way to understand their place in the world. They wanted to learn from his example.

Jesus didn't have a manifesto, and he couldn't refer someone to a book or an existing philosophy or say, "To learn more, read my book." No, his message spread because of his deeds, because of what he *did*. And people didn't follow him because he was labeled a Christian. They followed him because he embodied a new *way* to lead life that elevated individuals and gave them the freedom and responsibility to act. Individuals had a role—they were no longer idle passengers on the faith train. They had to love their neighbors and even love their enemies. Jesus meant love as a verb, a supremely powerful verb. And he made it crystal clear his own actions would show them exactly what he meant: "Love one another *as I have loved you*." He essentially said, "Watch me! Do as I have done. Live like I have tried to live."

To make their corner of the world better, his followers had to follow his lead and *act!* Jesus found disciples eager to do their part.

I believe, at heart, Americans today are just as eager.

That morning's speaker noted how the life and teachings of Jesus can be a guiding light for anyone in the world regardless of their religion or beliefs. Jews, Muslims, Hindus, Buddhists, and atheists can all follow the teachings of Jesus and not violate any tenets of their own system. Born-again evangelicals and used-to-be-Christians can likewise find value in what he taught.

People may not like Christians, the church, or Christianity, but it's hard to find fault with what Jesus showed us. Who could argue against following his lead?

The concept that Jesus wasn't a Christian meant to me that his actions mattered more than any doctrine or any words. The concept transformed my faith. I began to think of myself more as a "fan of Jesus" and less as a Christian beholden to the teachings and rules of any one church.

I felt no need to walk into a room and put my faith on display with my words. I was determined to display it with my actions.

Loving your neighbor became more and more achievable to me. I began to concern myself less with what the church said and more with what Jesus *did*.

And I found a better way to talk with people. I stopped framing things in the wording of the Bible or the politics of the church. I started speaking about living out values on which everyone can agree.

Jesus sparked one of history's most unlikely coalitions. The religion of Rome, tribal religions, and the religions of other civilizations mimicked the social order of their respective societies. They left the oppressed no less oppressed and the elite no less elite. My pastor beautifully frames how Jesus created a new order. He raised up individuals and put them on equal footing: Merchants and noblemen were children of God. Slaves and masters were children of God. And perhaps most audaciously for his times, he claimed women were children of God too.

Jesus preached that all were equal in his Father's eyes and we should treat each accordingly.

From that foundation grew Christianity. Even though followers of Jesus were persecuted and killed for centuries thereafter, the coalition grew. Generations of disciples (which just means students or learners) continued to honor and love one another. They practiced caring for their enemies. They carried one another's burdens and found understanding.

If they followed Jesus's example at the risk of their families' lives, we don't have much of an excuse for not following that example, do we?

Worst case, we lose some friends on social media, and we probably don't see them anyway.

You don't have to call yourself a Christian to grasp this example. You don't have to believe in a higher power to understand the point. History shows a man named Jesus started this unlikely movement and he can serve as inspiration regardless of your views. A scrappy rabbi unified an extraordinarily diverse group of people around the idea of loving one another as equals. He consequently set into motion one of the world's most influential, diverse, enduring, and widely joined journeys.

Religion should never be at the center of politics, but the lessons Jesus taught should be.

We need his example to heal today's broken politics because nobody else is big enough to solve our problem.

We don't need Jesus to promote this or that policy. We need him to show us how to function as a nation because it seems we've forgotten. We have never been perfect. There's no "great" past era to which we can all return and find harmony and happiness. We don't need Jesus to lead us back to some nostalgic golden age. We need Jesus to show us the path forward because we can't stay where we are for much longer.

Something has broken in our communities and in our politics. And I don't think it's the fault of our Constitution.

★ ★ ★

Americans have become isolated and lonely, and a host of forces are to blame for the brokenness we're experiencing.

In his book *Them*, Ben Sasse makes some great observations about how economic and social changes are compounding to put Americans on ever-smaller social islands. More people work alone; fewer people join clubs, churches, and organizations; more families are less stable; we move more often; and we know fewer of our neighbors. As a result, many of us now seek connection and identity in virtual tribes instead of local neighborhoods. We've let virtual communities—and often residential bubbles too—isolate us from different viewpoints and different people. We learn exactly one side to every story, and our interest in learning any *other* side is waning considerably. Even if we *want* to learn about the other side's perspective, we have precious few friends in our circles who might enlighten us. Information isolation makes our loving hearts vulnerable to fear, greed, and anger. Those emotions drive out hope, generosity, and love. We are facing a national spiritual crisis and no political policy or political reform can cure it. It just can't.

Our crisis is not one of belief. It is one of practice.

Pew Research reports 79 percent of registered Republicans are Christians. No crisis of religious belief here! A huge and active segment of the party make following the teachings of Jesus a central part of their lives. Following his example defines their faith. That's terrific, right?

In one way, yes. But when I look around, I see lots of division and rancor in our party. I hear good-versus-evil narratives. I hear about love but too often I don't see it given; I don't see Republicans using it in action. Disparaging "liberals" and demonizing fellow Republicans who disagree with us is not loving our enemies. Spreading misinformation for personal gain is not loving others. And if we let others do these things unchecked, we aren't loving them, either. Anger, greed, and dishonesty will rot their souls and those closest to them will bear the brunt.

I love that we're a party that celebrates faith. I just want us to practice it more.

My pastor tells how, at the end, Jesus prays for unity among his disciples, those twelve who ministered with him and the countless followers he hoped would join this movement. He knew he'd be dead in a matter of days and unity—*unity*—was foremost in his heart: "I pray that they will be one."

Now, when's the last time twelve people were unified on everything? I am *positive* the twelve disciples had plenty of disagreements among them, political and otherwise. Some might even line up close to today's Democrats and Republicans. And I bet Jesus knew it.

He also knew that only by being unified would his disciples and followers have the ability, and the credibility, to exemplify how Jesus taught them to love others—and only if they lived out his example would people join their movement.

Many politicians on both sides call for unity, but they have trouble with the question "Unify around what?" We hear calls to come together around the pandemic, around first responders, around justice, around being American. But *none* of those things is big enough. Nor are they specific enough to unify a country as big and varied as ours. Those calls for unity don't tell us what is expected of us, and they fall flat.

People don't act—often because they don't know *how* to act.

We face a country changing and growing as rapidly as any other in history. The small homogenous republic our Founders knew is gone. But remember, a crisis of unity came to that much smaller nation too. Civil war erupted less than 80 years after our founding, when 35 million people lived in 34 states. Today we are trying to coexist peacefully and respectfully in a country of 50 states and nearly 350 million people of all faiths, colors, perspectives, and backgrounds. The only other coalition ever this diverse in America? Christianity.

At least as I see it through my personal lens, leadership around unity falls to the example of a big-hearted carpenter named Jesus. His acts and lessons teach me three things: How to Understand, How to Love, and How to Forgive. Here's how they each inform me and might inform us as a party and a nation too:

1. HOW TO UNDERSTAND

Imagine two college students, a Republican and a Democrat, who are part of the nearly 40 percent of today's college students surveys reveal believe the other side is essentially evil. Now imagine they're marooned on a tiny island together for three months. I bet they'd disagree on policy just as much on Day 90 as they did on Day 1. But with 90 days to learn about each other, I firmly believe neither would think the other aimed to destroy America.

"Coming together" or being unified doesn't mean agreeing. But it *does* mean understanding.

Look, we can disagree bitterly on the means, but we can't let ourselves disagree on the ultimate motives.

If we base our understanding of the other side on news reports from our often-biased sources, we will never, never see them for what they are: *fellow citizens*—fellow mothers and fathers—trying to make life better for their kids in the way they think best, based on their experiences.

Our pastor tells a story about Rufus Miles, who advised three presidents: Republican Dwight Eisenhower and Democrats John F. Kennedy and Lyndon Johnson. Along the way he coined Miles's Law: "Where you stand depends on where you sit."

A person's stance on an issue, he realized, often depended less on philosophy and more on experience and circumstance.

Philosophically, I think the conservative path is most often the best path, but there are times I see different solutions, because either I'm standing somewhere different or I've taken time to learn more and found a better way. Regardless, I won't accuse someone of corruption just because they make a different argument.

I'm not perfect, but I try to avoid attacking anyone's motives if I haven't put myself in their shoes. If I don't know where they've sat, I can't begin to have a meaningful discussion with them. If I haven't carried their burdens, I can't really claim to understand their perspective.

And that's my loss.

In a way, the expression "Walk a mile in another man's shoes" comes from a letter one of Jesus's followers, Paul, wrote to people who had begun to follow the teachings of Jesus in Galatia. "Carry each other's burdens," Paul wrote, "and in this way you will fulfill the law of Christ."

Jesus had a really simple law: "Love one another as I have loved you." We can't love someone if we don't understand them. And we can't understand them if we don't bear their burdens, if we don't walk a mile in their shoes. Both Paul and Jesus knew once we carried the burdens of others and walked in their shoes, we couldn't help but love them. Even if they were part of the "them" too many leaders tell us to fear and loathe. This is how we make our country and our politics better.

What would happen if we all stepped out of our bubbles and committed to knowing our neighbors even just a little better? Wouldn't that ultimately help our politics?

2. HOW TO LOVE

In his last State of the Union address, the former president said, "Love is what powers and sustains our country." He spoke of "the infinite depth of love that dwells in the human heart." See, it's *okay* to say the word—even for *Republicans* to say the word! I'm afraid we don't say it often enough, however, and we might apply it even less. In a party that currently seems preoccupied with power and strength, saying "love" may feel out of step. I know we all say the word at home, to children or grandchildren before bed or to a spouse before leaving for the day. Yet I worry we've become less willing to use the word out in the world, which needs love just as much as our family does. Isn't everyone the member of a family too? Not ours perhaps, but someone's? Let your light shine, as the saying goes.

Go love them.

I'm getting nervous too many Americans are putting limits on love. It seems we're applying it in fewer places and to fewer people.

It's okay to love your neighbor unless she's set on an agenda opposite yours.

It's okay to love your neighbor unless he says Joe Biden won. (I have some personal experience with this one.)

It's okay to show your neighbors grace unless they live outside your bubble, because then they're not really your neighbor and someone else is responsible for loving them.

I can handle it if people aren't saying "love your neighbor" just because they think it makes them look weak or too religious. I'll work to show a different example. What I have more difficulty handling is the possibility they're not saying "love your enemy" because they no longer believe it. Jesus himself suggested we love our enemies—and he showed us how.

Whether you think he was divine or not, we know he prayed for the people who persecuted him. His last act was to forgive them. And he chided his followers for just doing the easy work of loving those most like themselves. The hard work—and the work that really heals and moves—comes when we love someone *different* from us, someone we might perceive as our enemy. That's where real change happens—in us and them. That's our calling and our duty as people involved in politics; we live to change lives for the better. We may talk more about making America great, but isn't a country a vast assemblage of millions of lives, joined together on a common journey?

If we talk more about making *Americans* great, we'll make more progress.

There's a reason the concept of love is so prevalent in faith and life: It's so powerful. It's powerful in the personal sense, the way it drives parents to care or protect their children. It's powerful in its ability to spark understanding and heal personal relationships as well as whole societies. It's also powerful because it moves us to sacrifice for others.

Love doesn't always win battles. It didn't fill the hearts of the Alabama state troopers meeting Georgia civil rights icon John Lewis as he led peaceful marchers into Selma in 1965. Heavy batons and vicious words rained down on Lewis and his marchers. The day became known as Bloody Sunday. The late congressman and I often opposed each other politically, but we shared a state and a faith.

I know love made him walk across that bridge in Selma and love allowed him to forgive the people who beat him.

He had enough burdens to carry—he didn't want to carry hatred in his heart too. Every Georgian should be proud of John Lewis, even as many of us diverged politically.

During the 1960s, Lewis walked alongside two other great Georgians, Andrew Young and Martin Luther King Jr., both pastors. Love and the example of Jesus powered the civil rights movement, which fundamentally changed America. The movement's leaders knew that Jesus was big enough to move an entire society. The marchers of the 1960s looked to Jesus's example; they didn't respond to injustice with hatred. They loved their country so much, loved liberty so much, and loved their children and fellow citizens so much, they knew they had to respond with love too. It was the only weapon strong enough. Love won the war.

Today people of every race and background face a different crisis: the fraying of our communities and national fabric along with the rise of misunderstanding, misinformation, and darker forces. We need the example of Jesus—and we need to practice it—just as a determined band of Georgians did a half century ago.

Part of our spiritual crisis stems from isolation, right? In my experience, nothing brings people together like serving others. Maybe it brings together people with the exact same background. It might also bring together people with one perspective to help people with an entirely different point of view. It doesn't really matter. The act of showing up, getting out of our virtual worlds, and physically joining with friends or strangers to care for others can be transformative.

Scholars love to debate how to create community in today's era.

Really? It's no secret!

Frontier communities raised buildings together, and the Amish still have barn raisings. A barn raising doesn't just help one farmer and his family by building him a new place to store hay and shelter animals. It reminds the community they're living life together and that they have a duty to aid their neighbors. People bond when they work together toward a common end. They come to understand those *with* whom they work as well as those *for* whom they work. What church doesn't help their community? What Scout earns a top rank without leading a service project?

Let's stop complicating the answer to the question, "How do we create community in today's America?"

Just go help your neighbors carry their burdens—and help your enemies bear theirs too. Go care for them. Any given day in America, countless groups are serving others. I'd encourage you to go find one near you.

Now let me ask you a question: Who can love a person or family better: you and your community or the government?

I'm answering, "My community and me."

That's the conservative philosophy. That answer comes from my belief that we should have limited government, particularly when it comes to helping people.

"Loving people" does not just mean giving them a government program.

I know there are valuable roles for government in caring for citizens and communities, but as conservatives, we should want citizens to take the lead wherever we can.

Nothing is more conservative or Republican than helping others!

And here's the thing: If we don't help our neighbors, government will step in. So not only is serving others the right and loving thing to do, it also accomplishes a key political goal. It holds government at bay and empowers individuals and families; institutions such as churches, charities, and corporations;

and local groups to solve their community's challenges as they think best.

Nothing is more conservative than love.

3. HOW TO FORGIVE

Most of us have a story etched in our memory of someone forgiving us for something that we did wrong. We rarely forget what we did wrong, and we almost always remember being forgiven. That act of forgiveness heals a broken relationship and often creates a bond between two people, one that can be stronger than any bonds that existed before.

Sadly, the art of forgiveness has been lost in politics. Every slight becomes a mortal sin by one against another. Responses come hot and fast, and often on social media for all to see. There's no dialogue, there's no understanding or healing.

We might forgive family or friends or colleagues, but we're not forgiving anyone in politics!

Hey, elephants have long memories, but that doesn't mean Republicans should too.

I've seen too many senators lose friendships and the ability to be effective because of the position a friend or opponent took years ago on a particular issue. They won't forgive. They'll harbor a grudge. They'll seek revenge.

It's petty, it poisons the party, and it makes coalitions harder to build around good policy. Sometimes, an aggrieved politician would scuttle a great bill rather than let someone who wronged them succeed. Who loses? First, the people. Second, the grudge holder loses! Resentment eats up a good heart like a hungry termite devours wood. You will carry that emotion like a backpack full of bricks everywhere you go. It will wear you out and drag you down.

Think brooding and feeding that resentment won't affect the other important relationships in your life?

Many legislatures and many executive branches are full of people carrying these heavy backpacks. Sometimes I think they like the grudge. They don't want to forgive. But I hope in their hearts, they know they should.

On one level, it's always wise to forgive unkindness by giving love. It helps you move forward and can bring real healing and better perspective to the one who slighted you. I like to see the best in people, and I believe when people attack you, there's something else going on in their life that must be hurtful or difficult, so it's important to extend some grace. Imagine what burdens they might be carrying.

I spent lots of time reminding myself of that during those trying months after the 2020 election. That helped me get through the storm with my heart and spirit intact.

Sometimes I'll find that kind of loving forgiveness amusing, and I'm sure I'll have opportunity to practice it in the months ahead. Responding with love can confuse the person you forgive to no end! As an elected official, I've also developed a helpful tool: *intentional political memory loss*. It's somewhere between forgiving and just simply forgetting. And it drives my staff nuts. But it has allowed me to be far more productive than I would have been otherwise. I've just learned to move on and I try to encourage my team to do the same—sometimes they get more upset at our opponents than I do. And you've never seen a person more baffled than one you approach not long after they've blasted you in the press—and you talk about working together on an unrelated idea or piece of legislation. Our nation's problems are big enough that we can't let our own petty grievances hamper our work.

I'm not here to tell anyone how to forgive. I do my best to use intentional political memory loss, but I still struggle with forgiveness. Everyone does, especially those of us with a toe in politics. But I *am* here to say individuals in our party need to forgive one another and those on the other side or else we'll grudge ourselves right into minority status. Forgiveness is the only way to heal ourselves and our land, for both sides. As for me, I'm ready to move on and find partners—regardless of our pasts—and build up GOP 2.0.

I don't know of another instance of political forgiveness more significant than the grace extended by Abraham Lincoln in his second inaugural address, delivered shortly before the end of the Civil War. Generations have seen the first Republican president's words of healing inscribed on the north interior wall of the Lincoln Memorial. The last paragraph reads:

> With malice toward none, with charity for all, with firmness in the right as God gives us to see the right, let us strive on to finish the work we are in, to bind up the nation's wounds, to care for him who shall have borne the battle and for his widow and his orphan, to do all which may achieve and cherish a just and lasting peace among ourselves and with all nations.

The Union's victory was inevitable when Lincoln spoke those words. Still, more than 600,000 Americans had died. Politicians and citizens who'd remained in the Union wanted revenge. They were screaming for justice. Forgiveness was not foremost in many Northern minds. Abraham Lincoln stood against that political tide and emotional swell. Whether soldiers who lost their lives wore blue or grey uniforms, Lincoln knew they left behind farms, stores, and families. He extended grace to both sides; he spoke to the victors *and* the defeated. The war shattered lives. Survivors in the South needed compassion, not condemnation. Northerners needed an example of how to forgive, how not to let vengeance poison their own hearts.

The president of the United States and the commander-in-chief bravely and graciously extended forgiveness to those who fought against his armies. He extended compassion to the innocent families ripped asunder by death and total war. His graceful words and intention welcomed back Southerners, just as the father welcomed back the Prodigal Son in Jesus's famous parable.

What better example of understanding, loving, and forgiving your enemies? What better example of putting people over politics and healing a divided nation?

There's a term I like: *creative grace*. It means inventing ways to extend grace to others. It humbles the giver and the receiver. In his second inaugural address, Abraham Lincoln invented a new way to extend grace. I'm not aware of a victorious leader who won with such grace and so wholly forgave adversaries who had, in fact, started such a costly war. Lincoln's response to the Union victory was a supreme example of humility. After four years of bitter war, during which he lost a second of his four sons and nearly saw his country dissolve, Abraham Lincoln did not gloat. He did not utter harsh words. He did not praise himself. He simply wanted his nation to move past the war—and move past it together.

Humility and forgiveness are hard to separate. Forgiving others makes you humble. But to forgive someone else you need to be humble. I can't tell you which comes first but I can tell you they're both important.

Humble people don't attack others. They're not loud voices on social media or the news. They don't put themselves at the center of every decision. They take time to understand and genuinely help. They don't hold a grudge. Most importantly, without humility, people cannot extend grace. They lose the ability to forgive.

Suddenly the state of American politics is easier to understand.

For people involved in politics or just interested in it, grace may be looking past the way someone voted. Maybe humility is disagreeing with someone but still extending them kindness and respect.

Two particularly humble acts of leadership made deep impressions one me (in addition to Lincoln's). These two acts are symbolic but also deeply indicative. They're the same act: washing feet. Jesus washed the feet of his disciples. The leader of what would become one of history's largest religions and most sweeping movements got on his knees and scrubbed feet that spent every day in sandals that walked across dirty streets and filthy barnyards. He was there to serve those he led. Two millennia later, Pope Francis began his tenure by washing the feet of juvenile inmates. Each year, he washes the feet of others, often of those overlooked by society. He humbles himself. He sets a powerful example of servant leadership for his church— and all of us—to follow.

Whether or not you're Catholic or agree with his positions, you can appreciate that Pope Francis knows what Jesus knew: a leader's actions matter most.

Leaders in this vein have extraordinary capacity to love. They show us what we fundamentally need to heal our wounds and tie our communities together: forgiveness. It seems our bar for leadership has fallen in recent years and present times demand we raise it. We should expect—because Americans deserve—leadership grounded in humility, forgiveness, love, and understanding. We talk about these values in our faith-oriented conversations every day. We teach them to our children. We expect them in our families, neighborhoods, and places of work. We pray for them at church. Most of us try mightily to live them through our lives.

We desperately need these virtues practiced in our politics.

I certainly try to practice them and fail too often, but I never stop trying and my family never begins expecting less of me. And in this political era so full of anger and rancor, Republicans and Democrats need to forgive one another and move to understand each other. In our own party, moderates, conservatives, and those aligned with and against the president need to put aside our relatively narrow differences and love one another. Let's also show America we can love those who don't usually vote for us too. Our leaders need to provide the example.

If our party's leaders don't act out these values we cherish, and if they lead us away from the example of Jesus and Lincoln, shouldn't we think twice before choosing to follow them?

Shouldn't we begin to think something is fundamentally wrong?

Shouldn't we act, out of love, to change our leadership and alter our path?

7

★ ★ ★

THE POWER OF MORE

I'VE NEVER BEEN LONELIER THAN I WAS IN THAT SMALL INDUSTRIAL television studio, telling the world Georgia held a free and fair election.

I could count on one hand the number of elected Republicans who were standing up with me. Friends and allies had abandoned me or worse, turned on me viciously. The Georgia Senate had become a home for me, and I wondered how I'd feel when I returned. I contemplated being shut out by Republicans for saying the truth and shut out by Democrats because I was still a conservative.

Speaking into that unblinking camera made me feel like a small, quiet voice in the dark. *Will anyone hear me? Does what I say even matter? What difference can I make anyway?*

Part of me wanted to pack it up and just go home.

Today, many Americans feel that way.

We are tired of lies, tired of misinformation, tired of being riled up and manipulated, tired of being used, tired of not getting results from our officials, tired of seeing rancor grow and people hurt, tired of feeling lonely and like we don't matter.

The more sinister forces in our political system *want* us to feel utterly exhausted.

They want you demoralized.

They want you isolated.

They want you to be so tired you just lay in bed scrolling through your media feeds.

They'll be right there, feeding you more misinformation and creating an echo chamber that becomes harder and harder to escape.

It simplifies your world, if that's what you're going for: Your tribe is good—the other tribe is bad. Your tribe's leaders need your unquestioning support to save you from them. And if they don't deliver for you or if they disappoint you, just be glad it's them not delivering because the other side would deliver even less and act even worse. And at the end of a long day, they'll hit some enemies and give you some wins to cheer. It's an easy trap.

We are busy, hardworking people trying to raise families, balance budgets, and put food on the table—maybe save a little too. It becomes easy to fall victim to leaders and groups that peddle simple solutions, misinformation, and us-versus-them sports. It's easy to feel too tired or too daunted to break out.

And if we did shake off this engineered reality, would it even matter? What could *we* do to fix our country?

I believe we're all closet change makers—and we are all overwhelmed by the size of the change that needs to be made!

Listen, I've been discouraged too. I've wondered how in the world I can make progress when the odds are so stacked and the obstacles clearly too great. I felt like that when I was cold calling major league teams trying to get drafted. I felt like that when I pitched against the Mets' Johnny O and again when I started my first business. My feelings on my first day as a Georgia state representative weren't very different. Then I ran for lieutenant governor with less than 4 percent name recognition.

But I don't know if I've faced a more daunting situation than being a lonely voice speaking out for truth around the election in the face of my party's leadership.

I have always been the underdog, but underdogs keep scrapping. I've also been told underdogs just aren't smart enough to quit. So now I'm scrapping harder than I ever have before. I'm trying to bring a new perspective to a party at war with itself. I'm taking hard hits from the wealthiest Republican machine in history.

Think that's not daunting? I'm either a dreamer or a glutton.

We all feel helpless at times. We feel outnumbered and sometimes we are. We ask ourselves, *What can* we *do?* Then we wonder if we do something, will it really matter?

Sometimes we don't know the answer.

I've thought long and hard about this. How can the many shine a light in when a powerful few keep the curtains drawn tight?

How can our individual actions become a collective sunburst so big and bright that no curtains can keep out the light?

I landed on several actions that are completely doable, will make a tangible difference in our communities, and will really enrich our lives in the process! They can build into that brilliant blinding sunburst I imagine.

My family and I are committing to all three—we've promised to hold each other accountable. I hope you and your family might join us.

We can harness three powers that draw on other people: the Power of Two, the Power of Three, and the Power of More.

The first involves two people with opposing views beginning a safe ongoing conversation with each other.

The second entails us getting our information from at least three sources to make sure we hear different viewpoints.

The third power involves us volunteering to help others. Let's commit to helping more people than just ourselves.

Now, I know some people don't want to talk with a Democrat or hear different views—especially from news outlets that might be biased. But our country is sick and so are we. We need to take the medicine.

I don't think this is hard medicine to take. There's nothing complicated here, and I honestly think we will enjoy these journeys, perhaps very deeply so. I'm suggesting three steps we can each take independently to help us understand, love, and forgive. These steps will heal our families and communities. They'll bring healing to our circles of influence and rebuild our relationships. They'll help us practice our faith.

If enough of us can take these steps, and keep walking this path, I know brighter days will be ahead for our party and our country.

We will be the light that gets in through the cracks.

THE POWER OF TWO

The first day of the 2014 Georgia General Assembly, freshman state representative Dewey McClain sat down next to me. We were seatmates and fellow back benchers in the State House of Representatives. Like me, Dewey grew up playing sports. He spent more time than I did in the big leagues, however. He played linebacker for the NFL's Atlanta Falcons for four years. Dewey was more than twenty years my senior, so I bene-fitted from his wisdom and enjoyed his good stories. A special friendship developed, even though he was a Democrat and I was a Republican. We disagreed on many partisan issues, but we'd always talk about the vote.

Listening to him unpack his perspective always made it a little harder to vote against him. I realized very quickly that Republican caucus talking points rarely painted a complete picture. I also like to think understanding my perspective made it a little harder for him to vote against me. But he usually did anyway! We often canceled each other's votes. Still, we'd always laugh and get along afterwards.

To this day, Dewey remains even more surprised than I am that I became lieutenant governor. He comes to visit me in the senate chamber when he can. He always reminds me of the line he repeated so often when we served in the House together: "What's right is right, and what's wrong is wrong." There's nothing partisan about that.

Here's my point: I had a friend on the other side. I found someone I could talk politics with—and disagree with!—safely. We could help each other understand where we sat and how we saw issues differently.

Sometimes we'd soften each other's positions. Other times, we'd just leave the other with a better understanding of our own thinking.

Those relationships are becoming too rare in legislative bodies and in communities and neighborhoods everywhere.

That separation only fuels our isolation and erodes our ability to empathize and understand.

My challenge to you is this: Find a someone with whom you disagree politically.

Commit to one another that you can openly discuss politics without letting disagreements end your relationship.

If things get too hot, stop the conversation and cool off.

Neither of you should expect to change the other, and that's not the point.

The point is to *understand* the other.

That's the Power of Two.

THE POWER OF THREE

Get your news from at least three sources. Pick your favorite conservative outlet then two others that are widely respected and considered more unbiased (at least relatively). Staying informed locally is important, too, so don't forget to have a local source that's widely read and respected. And please do not be part of cancel culture and stop following one outlet because you don't like one story or one opinion piece.

I know other people will have different views than I do!

Sometimes they're absolutely right—sometimes they just have a different take on an issue or event.

We *need* to hear other voices. It often helps us see the value of our own views. Other times, it helps us adjust our positions to be even stronger. And still other times, listening to other views simply helps us better understand our neighbors even if we never end up agreeing with them.

Gallup and the Knight Foundation released a survey related to media bias that might provide some reference points as you think about where to get your information.

MOST UNBIASED NEWS ORGANIZATIONS, RATED BY AMERICAN ADULTS

2018 Knight Foundation / Gallup survey

ALL AMERICAN ADULTS	REPUBLICANS	DEMOCRATS
1. PBS News	1. Fox News	1. AP
2. AP	2. *The Wall Street Journal*	2. PBS
3. NPR	3. Vox	3. ABC
4. *The Wall Street Journal*	4. Breitbart News	4. NPR
5. *USA Today*	5. PBS	5. CBS

MOST BIASED NEWS SOURCES, RATED BY AMERICAN ADULTS

2018 Knight Foundation / Gallup survey

ALL AMERICAN ADULTS	REPUBLICANS	DEMOCRATS
1. Fox News	1. CNN	1. Fox News
2. Breitbart News	2. MSNBC	2. Breitbart News
3. MSNBC	3. *The New York Times*	3. *Mother Jones*
4. HuffPost	4. *The Washington Post*	4. HuffPost
5. CNN	5. NBC News	5. Vox

It's really an easy step to take. Just check out more than one source. You might raise an eyebrow at headlines you'll see, I admit—I sometimes do. But that can be a good thing.

You'll quickly discover there are different perceptions of reality out there. You may even wonder if two outlets are covering the same story or same country. I found nobody is 100 percent on-target. Nobody has a monopoly on the real, full story. Every outlet has its bias and angle.

By looking across several sources, however, I can stitch together a story that seems close to accurate. And the story I settle on rarely lines up completely with the views of one side or the other. It takes a bit more effort, but it feels good to think independently.

I found the air smells pretty sweet outside the echo chamber, even if you just breathe it for a few minutes.

THE POWER OF MORE

Our family lived in Forsyth County for several years—and they were busy years. I started a company and Brooke became involved too. Like many Americans in that career-building phase of life, we were also building a family. Three growing boys needed our attention just as much as the business. We struggled to find the right balance, just as most parents do. We'd both flop onto the couch together after our last son was in bed. We were usually too spent to work on the business, which had an insatiable appetite for our time.

We'd think, *How did we make it through the day—and can we do it all over again tomorrow?*

We lived between home, youth sports fields, nearby office, nearby public schools, and church. Without realizing it, we'd entered one of American society's pleasant yet limiting bubbles.

The year before I first ran for the Georgia House of Representatives, our small group worked a shift at a food pantry. I can talk about that small group of mine all day long.

Now, I don't care what your faith is, but I'd encourage everyone to find a circle of people with whom you can meet weekly or monthly and just live life together. The relationships we cultivated in that group and the accountability we found there have transformed the Duncan family. The group's decision to serve at the food pantry is an example of this.

I'll be honest: I thought a food bank would have to be a long way away from my home. Or if it was nearby, it would have to be a warehouse that sent food to where people needed it. I never imagined anyone in our area was going hungry.

The food bank turned out to be closer than I'd ever imagined.

The first time we served dinner there, we worked a long shift with our small group members and two of our kids, whom we brought along. At 6 p.m., the doors finally opened. I walked outside and saw a line wrapping around the building.

I was stunned.

Perhaps that should be shame on me, but I just didn't know! I'd inadvertently slipped into that comfortable bubble.

Well, now I knew: Just a few miles from my house, people were hungry. People who lived just around the corner, but on a street I never passed, couldn't afford to buy food for their families.

Volunteering opens your eyes.

Sometimes it informs your view of the world and at other times, it changes your view of your own neighborhood.

Think about it: Volunteerism is the core of conservatism. We want to minimize government because we think private organizations and individual citizens can do many things better. If we're serious, then we have to step up and serve. We have to provide the solutions to our community's problems. If we don't, a smaller government won't be able to keep people from falling through the safety net (and we can't accept that), or a bigger government will pick up our slack.

If you and your neighbors aren't involved (and if my neighbors and I aren't involved either), the conservative model won't work.

That said, I *am* in government after all, so I'll share an ambitious idea to boost this concept of volunteerism: I'd like to see tax credits provided for volunteer hours given to areas of most-pressing need as a catalyst to experience how rewarding and recentering volunteering can be.

I tried including this concept in my rural healthcare bill, which would pass unanimously and create a tax credit for corporations and citizens who donated to rural hospitals, which were categorically in severe crisis. I knew some members of those communities didn't have dollars to donate but did have time, and I wanted them to be part of the solution too. I hoped to give them tax credit for hours they donated to rural hospitals.

Now, some will argue that people shouldn't be paid for volunteer work, and I understand that argument. Tactically and realistically, however, many people in rural communities make many tough choices, and we should make volunteering an easy one.

Let's not make volunteering solely a privilege of those not worried about putting food on the table.

Beyond that, I'm a conservative and I believe incentives matter. Why not give incentives that would help volunteers as well as the communities they're willing to serve with their time and unique talents? If serving others is healing—and I believe it is—I want as many people serving as possible. The good outcomes are worth every dollar of tax credit.

In the end, legislative committees and state agencies could never agree on a formula for awarding tax credits for volunteering and a way to ensure integrity. The idea wasn't included in the rural healthcare bill and I think Georgia missed a tremendous opportunity to unleash the power of individual citizens and communities.

I haven't given up, however.

★ ★ ★

It's sometimes hard to feel like we're making a difference by serving at a food bank or cleaning up a riverbank—the problems of poverty or conservation are so massive. But America is pretty massive too. We have nearly 350 million people. And if we trust one another to each do our part, all these individual actions—cooking breakfast for disaster victims, building a home for a family, reading to children in poor communities—will come together like so many rivers and swell into a conservative movement for citizen-driven change as massive as our challenges.

If we as a party can focus on helping Americans—and helping Americans help Americans—I'm convinced we can lift up this country and our party along with it. Our political challenge is finding the right policies to affect change, communicating in the right way, and making sure we truly understand our duties, our collective challenges, and our fellow Americans.

8

***

THE 4CS:
CHURCHES, CHARITIES,
CORPORATIONS,
AND CITIZENS

Since 2005, Republicans have led the state of Georgia. We haven't led perfectly, but we have a record that shows what conservative policies have done during a decade plus of Republican executive and legislative leadership.

We balanced our budget each year.

We were one of only a handful of states to have AAA bond ratings from every agency.

Just like most households, we made hard choices to make income equal expenses and investments. Granted, our constitution requires a balanced budget, and by the way, we should mandate the federal government balance its budget too. Fiscally, the United States is nowhere near close to having that conversation but we should work towards it.

I'm very proud that today, each Georgian owns just $1,216 of what little debt we do have in Georgia, which is related to bonds, not deficits. Only Nevada and Tennessee have less state debt per capita. The citizens of most states have per capita debt burdens that are double, quadruple, or even nearly ten times that of Georgia.

But think about this: After the recent administration and Washington Republicans and Democrats *doubled* the federal deficit, your share is now a whopping $85,000.

So whenever Republicans or Democrats from other states or the federal government suggest how we should run Georgia, you'll understand why I'm skeptical.

Low debt, fiscal responsibility, and conservative policies have fed a voracious economy in our state. *Site Selection*, a top economic-development publication, named Georgia as having the best climate for business for the last seven years. It named us the #1 state for doing business for the last six years. Only three states have higher rates of new business startups per month.

More business means more jobs, which means more stability and prosperity.

I'm not saying Georgia doesn't have work to do—we do—but we certainly have our economic engine humming.

We created the nation's top film-production industry and fueled it with our non-union climate, new training programs delivered via our community colleges and universities, and concerted outreach to investors. The General Assembly passed a generous tax credit that brought studios and film operations from across the country to our state, leading to billions in new investment and thousands of new jobs.

Stick around for the credits after the next film or series you watch—there's a good chance you'll see our Georgia peach logo at the end.

Democrats and Republican all worked together to realize this vision.

We're particularly proud of our higher-education system. An independent board of regents keeps politics out of education, so we can prioritize good policy and student outcomes.

That's policy over politics once again.

The board's data-driven work has led to Georgia being the only state besides California to have two public universities in the top 15: the University of Georgia and the Georgia Institute of Technology, better known as Georgia Tech, where I played baseball years ago. The Marlins drafted me before my senior year, so when I finally go back and finish my degree at Tech one day—and I will—I'll be attending a much better school than Tech was when I left!

We've raised the caliber of Georgia's schools and workforce with the HOPE Scholarship, a program funded by the state lottery that pays full or partial tuition for Georgia students attending in-state public colleges and universities or technical programs. A Democratic governor, Zell Miller, implemented the program, which parents in all political parties heartily support—especially those of us with children in college or headed in that direction. Before the HOPE program began, neither UGA nor Georgia Tech was ranked as top schools. Our student graduation rates for post-secondary and technical colleges have also risen: 10 percent in 10 years.

In Georgia, leaders of both parties have tried to prioritize good economic policy over flashpoint issues. We've had to follow the policy-over-politics philosophy as we've solved problems without using government alone. Other players such as churches, charities, corporations, and citizens who don't care about politics keep us focused on the real problems and real people. They won't tolerate the politics. We've in turn engaged them via successful bipartisan private-public partnerships that have yielded terrific results.

I am a believer in the ingenuity and problem-solving ability of institutions outside government. I always have been.

★ ★ ★

Earlier I mentioned I would have never run for lieutenant governor had it not been for the 2016 election. That was only half the equation. Georgia's healthcare crisis—playing out in rural areas in particular—was the other factor.

After several years at the state capitol, I began realizing hospitals and medical facilities across rural Georgia were in crisis. Really, many were failing outright in terms of finances and quality of care. Hospitals found it increasingly hard to serve rural populations, which tended to be poorer and dispersed, while also balancing their financial books. A big reason was reimbursement rates for private and public coverage were often too low to cover costs. When hospitals closed, local towns and patients lost access to healthcare, which fed a downward economic spiral. The hospitals' crises were their communities' crises, and any community's crisis is ultimately a family crisis.

I heard heartbreaking stories from real people from Georgia's many rural counties.

New representatives like me weren't yet jaded or afraid to dream big. I wondered how some combination forces and entities outside government might tackle this crisis.

The government certainly hadn't figured it out, and these people needed help. Yesterday.

In some ways it was natural that I would get involved in rural healthcare. Even though I lived minutes away from one of the state's best medical facilities, I'd traveled enough backroads on team buses to know real people faced real problems far from cities.

Now that I'd begun to understand the scale of the problem, I had to do *something*.

And I thought I might have an idea that'd work.

What if the state gave a dollar-for-dollar tax credit to companies and citizens who made donations to rural hospitals? If someone donated $100, they'd lower their Georgia tax bill by $100. Government wouldn't direct their dollars, tell hospitals how to spend the dollars, or use fifty cents of each dollar for the bureaucracy. People would pick the recipients and the recipients could use the money how they decided best. The state wouldn't attach strings or siphon off funds.

To me, it sounded like everyone would win.

Late one January afternoon in 2016, I dropped the bill into the hopper. I was still a no-namer in the House. My nearly seventy-year-old dad was my intern; I had no staff. I wasn't sure the Republican leadership could even pair my face with my name on the roster.

The next morning, they knew me.

I felt like the most popular legislator in the capitol. The governor eventually called me into his office, and I found myself in my first meeting with Georgia's chief executive. He lectured me on healthcare for ten minutes, basing his arguments on his time in Washington as a U.S. congressman. Then he asked me to explain my position.

In the interest of honesty, I noted the tax credit would be $250 million spread out over several years. He just looked at me.

He asked, "Why in the *world* would you ever ask for a tax credit this big?"

I looked back at him and said, "Because the problem is this big."

He nodded his head thoughtfully and stood up. The meeting was over, and we shook hands. Like a scene from a movie, he called my name as I walked out. "Geoff," he said. "If you need any help passing this bill, let me know."

Versions of the bill went back and forth between House and Senate. My father, still my intern, shuttled versions back-and-forth. In the end, the bill passed unanimously, and we've continued to improve it.

We tackled a serious problem by empowering corporations and citizens to help their local hospitals in new ways that sidestepped government. The private dollars flowed and hospitals were better for it. I'm convinced Republicans in Washington and each state can make progress on rural healthcare, maybe in a similar way, but that's up to them.

We've found success in Georgia by using a policy lens that includes Churches, Charities, Corporations, and Citizens, a lens I adopted shortly after being elected. The lens has become a powerful problem-solving paradigm I call the 4Cs.

THE 4CS
CHURCHES, CHARITIES, CORPORATIONS, AND CITIZENS

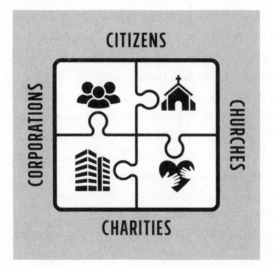

Georgia's Churches, Charities, Corporations, and Citizens are its greatest public-policy assets. These four groups have the talents and resources to bring a scalpel to work with them every day instead of the chainsaw often found inside government programs and agencies.

Government allocates funds because that's its job and reason for existing—or expanding. Churches, Charities, Corporations, and Citizens allocate funds because they choose to do so and because they truly believe in the benefits. They'll frequently offer more than their checkbook when they get involved. They bring awareness, innovation, efficiency, volunteerism and, most importantly, an exit strategy. Like a great hospital, they want to stabilize, treat, rehabilitate or cure, and release. They want to fix a problem long-term, not keep people on life support or make them permanent dependents.

Government has one big lever that is relatively easy to pull, as long as you have the votes. Create a program, allocate dollars, and distribute. Pretty easy. Leveraging the 4Cs takes more thought, time, and diplomacy. That can be a barrier in our busy world. But since when is the easy path the best route?

Identifying ways to involve these four assets takes thought, study, and coalition-building. I have seen fruits from this approach here in Georgia so I know it can be done; it just takes imagination, patience, and leadership.

Oh, and an ability to put policy over politics.

Leaders in these outside entities won't put up with politics. They're interested in solving problems efficiently and quickly. They keep our representatives and senators honest and focused on the people. Adoption, foster care, mental health, healthcare for low-income individuals, homelessness, infrastructure, technology, and training are several areas where the 4Cs, coupled with enabling legislation, can bring positive long-term change.

There will always be a role for government, but I'd rather it not be the *leading* role. Putting "We the People" in charge by using Churches, Charities, Corporations, and Citizens is the best way to help communities and families thrive. Just imagine the scale and scope of what the 4Cs could accomplish at state and federal levels if everyone could get a dollar-for-dollar tax credit up to 5 percent of their tax liability for donating to a verified worthy cause in their community.

I like to empower people, not government.

I love unleashing the power of individual care and ingenuity, not of government bureaucracy.

I prefer using effective private dollars to less effective government dollars.

I like to see people take responsibility for their community's future.

Using the 4Cs model is one of the best ways to realize these visions.

PART THREE

THE PET PROJECT

In Georgia, I've seen how individuals and institutions can work together to create and implement policies that benefit everyone. I've seen how deeper understanding and a gentler tone lead to outcomes that benefit families and entire communities.

*I'd like to share my views about how conservative **P**olicy, genuine **E**mpathy, and respectful **T**one (PET) are the Republican Party's ticket to reclaiming the majorities and respect these past years have cost us.*

9

★ ★ ★

POLICY

ON MY FIRST DAY IN THE GEORGIA HOUSE OF REPRESENTATIVES, I couldn't have told you what a policy wonk was, but I quickly discovered most representatives were either policy guys or political guys. Well, I soon learned I had no natural instincts for politics, so I became a policy guy by default.

By "soon," I mean eight days.

A vote came up for a bill levying a new tax on hospitals— it would be among my first votes. The Republican governor marshaled his troops behind the bill, but I thought it was bad policy—and it certainly wasn't conservative. I became one of 18 House members out of 180 to vote "No."

Now, I didn't know the other 17 representatives in hot water with me very well, but I definitely wanted to get to know them better. They became some of my closest friends, representatives with whom I'd spend countless hours in similarly hot water with party leadership, fighting for good policy over politics.

After that vote and several others, I became known as one of the most conservative members of the Georgia House when it came to policy.

Unbeknownst to me at the time, my "No" vote on that hospital tax would become one of my better political assets six years later when I ran for lieutenant governor.

I tell the Georgia Senate this every day: *If you get the policy right, it makes the politics easier.* Some representatives and senators thought I was naïve when I first said that, but now the vast majority on both sides of the aisle believe me and we've worked together to make real progress for real people.

One great example comes from a bill I co-sponsored that moved the ball on solar energy without using taxpayer dollars. Two of my colleagues spent a year negotiating with dozens of different players in the solar-power and electric-utility industries to find a way to legalize solar installations at residences and small businesses. The detail and complexity astounded me, yet the outcome was such good policy that it passed the House and Senate unanimously! Nobody made a single change. Perhaps even more amazing, not only were Democrats and Republicans working together on a conservative policy, even the solar lobbyists and utility lobbyists were getting along!

Good policy made the politics easy, and Georgians got a win.

Now, I'd be lying if I said politics don't matter. Of course they do—it's how good policy often gets passed. Passing legislation also requires numbers. It requires votes and coalitions. When your coalition is big, you accomplish goals. When your numbers are small, you don't.

Republicans used to understand this.

Dwight Eisenhower and Ronald Reagan united Republicans behind a conservative vision that connected with ordinary Americans. Ike won by 7 million and 9 million popular votes in 1952 and 1956. In 1980 and 1984, Reagan won by 8 million and 17 million. How did Reagan win over all those voters? Remember the "Reagan Democrats?" The Great Communicator reached across party lines and welcomed people who were with him on *many* issues, not *all* issues. And he made them feel part of the movement. Reagan built a massive coalition. Like their policies or not, both these administrations got things done because they had numbers.

Our most recent former president, on the other hand, left us with "Biden Republicans."

Since Ronald Reagan's 1986 landslide, the GOP's national margins have shrunk along with the diversity of its coalition. Broadening the party's appeal is the only way to reclaim true national mandates so we can pass effective policies. Doubling down on purity and the base cost the party dearly in 2018 and 2020. And we can't expect more turnout from our base than we saw in 2020—and remember, the demographic groups in the GOP base are shrinking, not growing. We must build a larger coalition.

Look, there will always be different views and goals within both parties, and nobody is getting everything they want. Really, don't we teach this to our kids? In life we almost *never* get everything we want, so we shouldn't expect that in politics of all places.

Let's remember politics is "the art of the possible," the art of gathering votes from different pockets to make progress. We might create one coalition for this issue and another coalition for that issue. We may get much of what we want on one bill, and less on another. But we'll make progress and that's good for our constituents, which is the most important thing!

Imagine what might be feasible if we keep that in mind.

Now, what if the GOP finds a handful of conservative policy issues on which a significant majority of Republicans and most Americans agree?

If we did that, we could hammer out legislation that would pass locally and nationally.

Let's accept the inevitable compromises, let's even make it bipartisan, like we did in Georgia with rural healthcare and hate crimes. Then let's celebrate outcomes that will help the people who elected us—and like it or not, those outcomes will help those who voted for our opponents too.

I got booed for suggesting that idea at the president's November 2020 rally, but I said those words countless times on my own campaign trail and conservatives would cheer: "Our policies are so good they even help people who don't vote for us!"

★ ★ ★

In this out-of-power season, it will be easy for national Republicans to become the party of "No."

It's always easy to say why the majority has a bad idea.

It's easy to snipe from the back bench.

It's also easy to avoid putting forth your own good ideas.

We can't let our national leaders fall into that trap. It's bad for our country—we need good conservative policies to be debated and passed. Further, being branded as obstructionists nationally hurts Republicans locally. We state-level folks carry enough national baggage as is. Nationally and locally, we must be a party of ideas. We must be a party that gets things done for the people.

Following that, I want to talk about policies where the GOP can build trust inside our party, grow support among independents and moderates, and pass legislation that helps real people. There will be many, many areas for disagreement among members of our own party and with those in the Democratic Party. But let's focus on where we can agree. As my coaches used to say, "Let's just get some runs on the scoreboard."

I've asked myself how Republicans might approach policy in a way that can unite our party, engage the vital middle, and deliver results that help Americans. How might we leverage the power of Churches, Charities, Corporations, and Citizens to help real people address real problems? I think it starts by finding a new framework.

I like one I'm calling the GOP 2.0 Policy Prism and it has three important facets.

One, let's double down on the conservative policies for which the GOP has always been respected. Two, let's be willing to have some difficult conservative conversations, where we can address complicated issues from a conservative perspective but seek to make progress. Leadership means being a grown-up and having the tough talks that need to be had. We owe that to our voters. And three, let's keep the innovative ideas flowing. We can think creatively about using assets and resources to solve problems—employing the 4Cs of Churches, Charities, Corporations, and Citizens—whenever possible.

GOP 2.0 POLICY PRISM

1. Brand Baseline
2. Conservative Conversations
3. Innovative Ideas

1. BRAND BASELINE

Republicans should never walk out of a room without people knowing our party is hands-down the best at growing the economy, ensuring public safety, and providing national security.

Economic Growth

We know—and conservative-led states such as Georgia demonstrate—that economies grow in climates with low taxes, with strong public education systems, and where there's investment and collaboration between the public and private sectors.

Republicans know small businesses are our country's lifeblood—and we've built a strong reputation as a friend to the small business community. America has 31.7 million small businesses, and they employ 60.6 million Americans, nearly half our national workforce. More than 5 million of them are self-employed minorities. The year prior to the pandemic, 2019, small businesses created 1.1 million net new jobs. That's an engine we want to keep running! Let's keep burdens low so leaders and workers can grow their businesses and create economic opportunity for themselves and others. We can be small businesses' best advocate.

Public Safety

For public safety, GOP 2.0 will embrace the role good policing and public safety play in our country.

We can find broad support for reforming the criminal justice system so we can keep the peace and keep families safe while also helping people avoid trouble in the first place and ensuring people are treated fairly, safely, and justly at every step. And when people do find themselves inside the system, we should find ways to equip lesser offenders with the tools and skills they need to make a better path for themselves *outside* the system. As long as safety permits, American potential doesn't need to be locked up or dragged down by inescapable cycles of fines and penalties.

Importantly, we shouldn't forget the honorable men and women who pin on a badge and serve, either. They have challenging jobs that require real sacrifice and come with danger. They put their lives on the line daily. We should be grateful and respectful, and we should help them do their vital jobs safely and well.

Republicans can make a promise to America's citizens: We will make your streets safer than they've ever been before. Parents are dog tired of worrying about their kids' safety—and their very lives! Parents in vulnerable communities understand that fear too well. All parents, especially those parents fighting poverty, too, have enough to worry about. Our party can address their challenges and lift up these individuals and families not just through economic policy, but through public safety policy as well.

National Security
Nothing else matters if our government gets national security wrong. Our nation's freedom and independence are paramount. Their preservation protects and enables all else we enjoy and value. Right now, falsehoods, conspiracies, and divisions are threatening that vital protection.

Republicans following the former president are doing serious damage to U.S. national security as they follow the Russian, Chinese, and Iranian playbooks by sowing unrest, mistrust, and near insurrection here in the United States. They accomplished in a few short weeks what our foreign enemies had been trying to do for years! Before we can expect people to listen to Republicans talking about national security, our party has to stop being a security threat itself.

Here in Georgia, we're proud to host military bases including Fort Benning, Fort Stewart, Marine Corps Logistics Base Albany, Moody Air Force Base, Naval Submarine Base Kings Bay, and Robins Air Force Base among others. Our bases support the U.S. Army's 3rd Ranger Battalion and 3rd Infantry Division, the Navy's Trident nuclear submarines, and the Air Force's 23d Wing. We also have corporations such as The Home Depot, Delta Air Lines, and UPS, which go extra miles to honor, support, and hire military veterans—an informal yet immeasurably valuable private-public partnership.

Georgia knows how to prepare, support, and appreciate those who serve. Our military families know the importance of a government that stands up to enemies. They understand the sacrifices needed to protect our country and its ideals—and they willingly make them. At the federal level, our government must honor those families and their servicemembers with policies that protect national interests by projecting force responsibly—and always with an exit strategy. Let's not dishonor these individuals and families by destabilizing our democracy with misinformation and distrust and thus aiding foreign powers. We need conservative international and military policies governing our relationships with other countries. We need a strong and nimble military always prepared to meet global threats as they evolve.

I want GOP 2.0 to win back trust and credibility with honesty and strength. When I hear a general or admiral say something, I'm pretty sure I can take it to the bank. People should respond to Republicans in the same way.

2. CONSERVATIVE CONVERSATIONS
Fiscal Restraint

Our country has a spending problem. A big spending problem. And Capitol Hill Republicans are just as much at fault as Democrats. Despite being in the party usually known for fiscal restraint, the former president and GOP congressmen and senators spent like mad, running up deficits and the national debt even as they controlled the Big Three during most of federal fiscal year 2017 and all of fiscal 2018. Then they lost the House and the deficits kept climbing—again, both parties are to blame.

I'll keep this really simple. Just review the following chart and you can see what happened to the idea of Republican fiscal restraint and our party's long-standing goal of controlling government spending. During this past Republican administration's one term, the old GOP deficit hawks barely make a peep.

FEDERAL BUDGET DEFICITS AND THE NATIONAL DEBT (2016–2021)

Source: Congressional Budget Office

FEDERAL FISCAL YEAR	FEDERAL BUDGET DEFICIT	NATIONAL DEBT
2016	-$584.7B	$12.2T
2017	-$665.4B	$14.7T
2018	-$779.1B	$15.7T
2019	-$984.2B	$16.8T
2020 (not including C-19)	-$1.0T	$17.9T
2020 (including C-19)	-$3.142T	$21.0T
2021	-$2.3T	$22.5T+

(Note: Federal fiscal years end September 30. Debt refers to debt held by public.)

If these numbers frighten you, that's because they should.

And it's time we had a conservative conversation about how we fix our financial house.

I don't advocate a knee-jerk slashing of spending, nor do I advocate a knee-jerk tax hike. Clearly, however, we have to fix this problem and do so in an honest and fact-based manner that's fair to Americans and keeps our economy strong. I'll be glad to talk with the politicians in Washington and share some lessons on how we balance budgets here in Georgia.

Healthcare

If you look at the data, a majority of voters rank healthcare as a top concern (68 percent). Feeling secure about accessing and affording the care you need is an *intensely* personal issue. Yet for a full decade, the main GOP policy on healthcare has been "repeal and replace Obamacare." At the end of 2020, 65 percent of independents and 62 percent of the overall population wanted to keep the Affordable Care Act or build on it—and a full 45 percent of Republicans supported some public-insurance option, as did 68 percent of independents.

Yet the same survey showed 87 percent of Republicans opposed "Obamacare."

A decade of sloganeering has sold a tagline but not a policy. We still haven't addressed constituents' real needs. We spent too much energy criticizing Obamacare versus bolstering good Republican alternatives. We gave voters a convenient scapegoat that helped us win elections ten years ago.

In 2018 and 2020, healthcare helped us *lose* elections.

We need a real policy.

Ironically, Republicans had the framework for one years ago. It was developed by the conservative Heritage

Foundation and implemented successfully in Massachusetts by then-Governor Mitt Romney. Almost everyone in Massachusetts gained coverage without the government running the show.

Then President Obama basically co-opted the program. Instead of collaborating to make good policy, the GOP derisively labeled the whole thing "Obamacare" and attacked.

We put politics over policy.

I'm not saying the ACA was or is the answer. It tackles an enormous sector and is fraught with issues and challenges, and we've seen them play out. Perhaps most glaringly, the cost of coverage has risen dramatically along with deductibles, so Americans are getting squeezed and still do not have better access to care. Promised competition among insurance providers hasn't materialized in many areas, either.

National GOP leaders have offered several alternatives, but none passed even with Republican control of the Big Three. We never gave real help to the Americans who needed it. We may have tried, but from where they were sitting, we didn't deliver. It cost us.

Healthcare is a major problem that still affects both parties and I guarantee you the answer won't be found in the extremes. It'll be in the middle, and I'm convinced voters will reward us for finding it. But we've got to have the conversation—and do so from a conservative perspective.

Immigration
Of all the issues facing us in the coming years, immigration will be among the most complex. It's a riddle that has eluded us for decades but it's high time we solved it. I don't pretend to have all the solutions. I do know that immigration policy will

take bipartisanship, honesty, and courage. I also know it needs two key components.

All the border security in the world doesn't really help if we can't address the 16-plus-million undocumented immigrants who live in the United States. And it doesn't really help the situation if we deal with the 16-plus-million undocumented immigrants living among us if we don't secure the border. Both fronts need our attention.

I get that immigration is a difficult issue—that's why immigration policy has vexed and eluded numerous administrations and that's why policy has been driven by executive orders more than congressional action. We can't keep putting off the issue. Too many lives are affected, and immigration is too central to the American story to let the current crisis fester any longer.

One in ten Georgians and one in eight Georgia workers is an immigrant and believe me, we value them and all the contributions and richness they bring to our communities. We also have an estimated 300,000-plus unauthorized immigrants living in our state. Of those, 21,000 are DACA (Deferred Action for Childhood Arrivals) recipients who came here as children. We want them all to be safe and we also want them to pay taxes—which many undocumented immigrants do. Nationally, they pay around $9 billion in annual payroll taxes.

We want to encourage positive contributions from immigrants and keep benefitting from new people coming to our country. But we need to fix the crisis at the border and our troubled system. And that means having conversations about immigration that lead to good policy. Republicans and Democrats have tried and failed before but it's time for legislators to do their jobs and act—to put policy over politics and stop using immigration as a wedge issue.

People, just work the policy problem!

In my mind, the solution involves securing our border using expertise and resources from an organization experienced in guarding some of the world's most dangerous borders: the U.S. military. We don't want the military helping manage the border because of their weapons. We want to leverage their experience, resources, and manpower.

"Build the wall" was a slogan, not a policy. We need a policy.

Those who've come to our country illegally as adults and who are contributing, tax-paying members of communities need a path to resident status or citizenship. The GOP isn't winning any friends by threatening communities or breaking up families with deportations. As Republicans, we tend to believe incentives matter, so let's give undocumented immigrants a pathway toward which they can work hard.

We also can't forget the international element of immigration reform. We should also ask how we can help address the root cause of so mass migration: unrest, danger, and lack of opportunity in many Latin American countries.

And Republicans, we must talk about immigration in a loving way. We're talking about people and families. Nobody is evil because they crossed a border to find work and feed their children. Nobody dreams of leaving their home and walking hundreds or thousands of hungry miles to a new country, where maybe—*maybe*—they gain entry and start working hard minimum-wage jobs. Nobody aspires to send off their children alone on an uncertain trek. As a parent, seeing children arrive at our border alone breaks my heart. We must have compassion and respect for immigrants and their communities here in America.

And you know what, many of these immigrants won't look like many of us. They may not speak the same language or have the same experiences. I realize that can be uncomfortable. But I come back to something I've experienced time and again. People will disparage immigrants or rail against illegal immigration—then they'll turn around and note how the immigrants they know personally are wonderful people. And I know more than one Republican who doesn't ask his hardworking yet inexpensive maintenance workers about their immigration status.

America is growing and it is changing. Immigrants will be a part of that, as they always have been. We really have no choice but to embrace those realities and ensure these new neighbors are brought into the economy so our GDP can grow and all communities can benefit. Republicans can lead on this if we talk about it smartly and compassionately.

Pro-life Criminal Sentencing
Another issue tugs at my heart here. The polling numbers don't support me yet, but it's a matter of time until they will.

It involves life. We need better healthcare to improve lives. We need laws that protect unborn children. Smarter gun policy will save lives in schools and communities.

Adopting pro-life criminal sentencing will protect life, even when it's the life of a criminal.

My journey on this issue began while I was working to pass pro-life legislation in the Georgia Senate. My boys came to me one night and asked, "Dad, why do you fight so hard to protect unborn babies but support the death penalty?"

They didn't mean to land a gut punch, but they did.

I have always understood the death penalty but the older I've gotten, the more I've questioned it. My boys made me examine the issue from another perspective.

As a man of faith, I've come to find peace in being pro-life across the board: abortion, healthcare, better gun policy, and capital punishment. That suits me. Many might disagree but as for the ultimate justice, I'll leave that to the Lord.

I also found the academic argument compelling. We know—*know for a fact*—that states put innocent people to death. We know capital cases are expensive and disproportionately brought against poor minorities. We know the death penalty is not a deterrent.

And if you look at the list of 53 countries that still execute criminals, trust me, you don't want our country to be on it.

I ache for any family that suffers a loss. I want justice done as badly as anyone. I just feel the ultimate justice lies in the Lord's hands, not ours.

In the end, I've come to believe it's time to repeal the death penalty.

It's right and electorally smart for the GOP to advocate for ending capital punishment at state and federal levels as part of broader criminal-justice reform. Fewer than half of non-whites support capital punishment. Fewer than half of those born after 1996 support it. We need to have conversations with them so we can engage their hearts, win their votes, and help them achieve their aims. Those growing groups represent future trends and groups our party needs to win long-term.

I see the challenges, but if we're willing to talk about it, I believe the GOP can lead on this issue, nurture a broad culture of life, expand our tent, and benefit from America's gradual shift on the issue.

Term Limits

Some friends joked that I ran for lieutenant governor because the office has no term limits.

So perhaps I spoiled my own comfortable future when I promised I'd serve two terms at most and would introduce legislation to term limit my office, which I did.

I didn't think anyone needed to be in the same job for much longer than a decade. You get stale, entrenched, and, frankly, too powerful. As years go by, you're more likely to cling to that ever-more-comfortable office and lose your spine, lose your willingness to do what's right if it might cost you reelection.

You also risk becoming less responsive to constituents as you feel more entitled and secure—and incumbent politicians are right to feel secure! In 2020, voters reelected 95 percent of state-level incumbents; 96 percent of sitting members of Congress won reelection. In 38 states, 100 percent of U.S. House incumbents who sought reelection won. The Founders never envisioned a political class who would make government a career by entrenching themselves in office. They never envisioned the sums of money now flowing into campaigns that are benefitting incumbents. Nor did they foresee the dysfunction and gridlock that gums up today's legislative chambers.

How might we bring new generations of citizen-legislators into the process?

How can we free at least some officials from the pressures of reelection so they might be more encouraged to put policy over politics more often.

I introduced legislation to term limit myself, and I'd suggest other Republicans consider doing the same. Fifteen states already have limits for their legislators. Other states, like

Georgia, can start at the state level, as the 1995 Supreme Court decision in *U. S. Term Limits v. Thornton* stands in the way of limiting Congressional or Senate terms.

Still, term limits are popular. Related referendums in those fifteen states passed by an average of 67 percent. Maybe our constituents don't like us as much as we think. Gallup's most recent polling shows a full 75 percent of Americans support term limits. The GOP can give the people a bipartisan win here.

I'll add that the conservative in me particularly likes a Florida State University study showing government spending and taxes in states with term limits grow at rates between 16–46 percent slower than other states.

Conservative Gun Policy

Republicans have stood firm for Second Amendment freedoms. I've stood alongside my fellow conservatives on this issue. Gun violence and mass shootings have convinced large majorities of Americans that we need better gun policy. Our party's hardline positions are increasingly out of step and voters will eventually punish us. If our Second Amendment position loses us our ability to win independents and moderates, it will cost us more elections and we'll lose even more influence than we lost in 2018 and 2020.

I'm arguing for better gun policy made by conservatives so conservatives can control the debate. If we don't move our feet at all, Democrats will own the debate entirely, and we'll get extreme gun control instead of better gun policy.

Today Republican voters talk about better gun policy all the time, but Republican politicians are under an effective gag order from the National Rifle Association and other special interest groups. Let's step up and talk about an issue that concerns real Americans. We can't entirely stop gun violence, but we can maintain control of the debate by taking smart steps that balance our freedom to bear arms with everyone's right to security.

My ideas here aren't entirely tactical. As a father and lieutenant governor, responsible for the lives of my three boys and 2.5 million other Georgia children, I believe conservatives can find ways to make our children and communities safer while still vigorously protecting our Second Amendment rights. When a school shooting happens and my kids ask me what I did to stop it, I want to have an answer. When I talk with them about the value of life, I want them to see my policy positions reflect that. So let's have a conservative conversation about better gun policy. Let's try to give America the conservative version of gun policy before we all get a far-less-conservative one.

3. INNOVATIVE IDEAS

In Georgia, we're talking about government *investing* instead of government spending.

The concept of private-public partnerships has helped us make that philosophy real—and it helped create bipartisan majorities too. Following the 4Cs approach to problem-solving, I've supported initiatives where private dollars can juice government dollars and where private entities can lead policy while the government simply enables it through legislation. We have used this approach to help Georgians more quickly, efficiently, and meaningfully than we could have if we'd used government alone.

Churches, Charities, Corporations, and Citizens are powerful forces.

Here's an example. Our state, like many others, struggles with foster care. As a representative, I discovered a veritable crisis. How could we improve the system? How do we help children as well as foster parents? How could we do it without expanding the existing government programs that didn't seem to be fixing the situation in the first place?

Georgia turned to Churches. The state now partners with faith-based communities to help children in foster care. For example, the United Methodist Church-affiliated Wellroot organization tells the state how many children it can support. The state then provides funding and volunteers, and children benefit.

Faith-based organizations are loving Georgia's foster children in ways government never could.

Private-public partnerships work in education too. Georgia's REACH program finds at-risk 10th graders, coaches them, and provides a college scholarship at graduation if the students stick to a performance contract they sign. REACH takes kids going nowhere, with no means of attending college, and puts them on a path to college—and puts them through college too!

Corporations and Charities match funding from public sources to make REACH happen.

Organizations such as Microsoft, Google, and Code.org have helped Georgia students develop the skills they'll need to compete in a tech-savvy workforce. In 2019, 0.5 percent of Georgia students took a computer science class. Given that technology will define Georgia's future, that had to change. I pushed a bill that provided funding to local districts so every school in Georgia could offer at least one computer science class by the 2024–2025 school year. Corporations provided training for free or at reduced costs to put us on track to meet the goal.

While we're discussing technology, I'll share a story about Brook's grandparents. They both worked at Eastman Kodak, the venerable film and camera company that once led across its markets. Then Kodak's leadership missed the digital revolution, and the company went out of business. It cost Brooke's grandparents their pension, it cost thousands of jobs, and it cost shareholders their equity.

I never want to be associated with a group that misses or fails to capitalize on a transformative or disruptive trend, and so I campaigned for lieutenant governor with a promise to make Georgia "The Technology Capital of the East Coast."

If you're not from Georgia, then game on.

We're aiming to make our state the best place to invest in technology, and I'll challenge every other state to join the race. We need fifty states innovating and learning from one another.

Every business in our state and your state is a technology business. Coca-Cola uses technology to deliver millions of bottles and cans around the world, our farmers use technology to improve crop yield, and supply stores in south Georgia use datamining to find their next customer. Schools in every community need access to technology, and they need technology education in their curriculum.

Technology may be the best lifeline for rural Georgia and rural America.

In Georgia, we created the Partnership for Inclusive Innovation, a private-public partnership that identifies real problems; finds new solutions or start-up businesses to address them; creates public-private partnerships to invest in the ideas; and accelerates development so we can send the idea to the marketplace to grow. Its board includes leaders from Georgia's largest companies and universities.

Among the things I'm most excited about? Using the Partnership to find ways to bring broadband technology to rural Georgia so people can grow new businesses and participate in the information economy from their homes in Georgia's wonderful small towns. In fact, our first grant aims to build a network of mentors and training programs for entrepreneurs in cities, towns, and rural areas outside metropolitan Atlanta.

We have to find ways to share economic success with smaller communities in Georgia and elsewhere. Technology bridges that urban–rural divide; it also bridges party divides.

Economic growth, opportunity, and jobs should be a bipartisan effort. Politicians need to stop hijacking them for partisan purposes.

Nobody should be left out of tomorrow's economy, and during 2020 and 2021 we saw the consequences of people of all backgrounds feeling left behind.

I'm sharing Georgia's example, hoping you can find lessons to help your own state. Where can you put policy over politics and help build up your state using the 4Cs?

★ ★ ★

As a minority party in Washington, Republicans should focus on finding ways to pass conservative legislation that makes sense and can muster support from a solid majority of Americans—and a majority in Congress. And we should be willing to be adults and have needed conversations about difficult but important issues. If we focus on the policy instead of the politics—and can get enough Democrats to do the same—we'll help real people. If we can all engage Churches, Charities, Corporations, and Citizen as problem-solvers, we'll help real people.

On the other hand, if Capitol Hill Republicans instead choose to be obstructionists and nothing more, then that dirty boulder will roll downhill and rampage through our states and local districts, smashing the credibility and potential of local Republicans. The Grand Old Party must become the party of ideas again and be smart enough to get those ideas passed into law.

Now let's talk about how we can ensure we're building the necessary coalitions and communicating our case more effectively.

10

★ ★ ★

EMPATHY

REPUBLICANS SHOULD NEVER ASK SOMEONE FOR THEIR VOTE without truly understanding why that person should vote for our candidates. How is it that our party will make their life better? How will our policies address their challenges? How will they thrive more under Republican leadership than under leadership provided by the other side?

Republicans needed a whole lot more empathy in 2020. Many people we thought would or should vote for us ended up voting for another party. We didn't reach out to them effectively. We didn't make time to meet them, understand them, and truly love them. We didn't carry their burdens. And we lost the Senate and White House as a result.

I'm convinced a different path, one marked by more understanding and genuine outreach, would have led to a different result.

★ ★ ★

Our state of Georgia needed lots of empathy in 2020 too. And we didn't just need the noun; we needed the verb. It seemed we'd almost forgotten how to empathize with one another. Then two Black Georgians were killed as the nation was grappling with racial injustice. These tragedies reminded us of the injustice experienced by too many, and it reminded me about the value of understanding points of view different from my own.

The vigilante shooting of Ahmaud Arbery in Brunswick, Georgia, and the police shooting of Rayshard Brooks in Atlanta deeply affected our state and its communities. These two shootings didn't happen in my neighborhood. I knew none of the people involved. The victims didn't look like me and we would have never crossed paths. How could I know what life was really like for them? It was hard for me to empathize, truly, with the victims or their families and communities.

Then I spoke with Ahmaud Arbery's mother. I had my team find her number and we talked over the phone as lieutenant governor to constituent—and as a father to a mother.

I won't share anything about the private conversation except that she taught me more about criminal-justice reform and Georgia's need for it than any book, article, or party position brief could have.

She was a mother who'd lost her son to a violent murder. Three men had chased down Ahmaud while he was jogging in their neighborhood. One of them struck him with a truck. Cornered, he fought for his life until multiple shotgun blasts to his chest stole it from him. His mother knew his killer had taunted him with a racial slur while he lay dying on the street, without her or anyone who loved him by his side. He essentially died alone, leaving an unfinished life behind him.

Imagine how that makes a mother feel.

It got worse for her. Police investigated. Prosecutors considered the evidence. No charges were filed.

More than two months later, a video of the shooting surfaced. Had it not been released to the public, no justice would have been served.

You see, three different prosecutor's offices declined to press charges against the killers. Only when the video surfaced did the landscape change.

Seventy-four days after the incident, the perpetrators were finally arrested, and justice began to be served.

Ahmaud Arbery's murderers would have walked free if their fate been decided by any of those three prosecutors. Luckily, the video moved the state to action.

If the next victim of a hate crime doesn't have the state intervene, I wanted to be sure that victim and his or her family could still get the justice and peace they deserved. Can you imagine losing a son to murder and then finding no recourse to justice? No mother should ever face that situation in today's America.

My family and I were under COVID-19 lockdown and watched the nation respond to the deaths of Breonna Taylor, George Floyd, Ahmaud Arbery, and other Black Americans. I began to look into how Georgia had responded and found we were one of only four states without hate-crimes legislation.

I wanted out of that club.

I thought Georgia, of all places, should lead on this issue. We carry the legacy of Martin Luther King Jr. and John Lewis, and I wanted us to live that out.

I'm a man of faith, and I did my best to view Georgia's situation through that lens. Jesus called on his followers to treat others as we'd want to be treated, to love others like he did. He also showed them how to stand up for the vulnerable, comfort the afflicted, and welcome the ostracized.

At heart, that's what I envisioned Georgia's hate crimes legislation accomplishing. And the policy reflected the values Georgians hold. We do not tolerate hate.

I discovered a related bill had been languishing in committee, stalled by internal political nonsense and finger-pointing. I had several interactions with the press, including a press conference, and declared passing bipartisan hate-crimes legislation a top priority. Republicans held majorities in the Senate and House, so I knew we could pass a bill. But I wanted to pass the *right* bill with Democratic support.

So I sat down with Democratic leaders in the House and Senate.

I asked my Black colleagues to help me craft legislation that would matter and pass.

I built friendships that would last long beyond that single bill, even though we went back to voting against each other on many other policies.

On this matter, we were allies. We built the necessary coalition. When the vote came, we had unanimous support from Senate Democrats. It wasn't easy, but patient dialogue got us there. All but a handful of Republicans voted in favor too. Since our coalition took hits from the right *and* the left, I thought we were probably on the right track. And we were indeed.

House Bill 426 passed 127–38 in the House. When I gaveled the vote closed in the Senate on June 23, 2020, the bill had passed 47–6. Every member of the Democratic caucus voted in favor; all but a handful of Republicans did too. The governor signed it into law soon thereafter.

Passing hate crimes legislation will always be one of my proudest moments because of the statement it made, the good it accomplished, and the bipartisan coalition we assembled to pass it.

In that moment, we put policy over politics.

Republicans learned to empathize with people who didn't necessarily vote for us. And Georgians are better for it.

By January 6, 2021, it looked like we needed just as much empathy in the new year as in the previous one. Tens of thousands of angry people rallied in Washington, DC, and many stormed into the U.S. Capitol. They had come to Washington for many reasons, and I think they all wanted to express some sense of anger and frustration. Some felt disenfranchised, like nobody represented them. Some felt their families had little opportunity. Some felt devoted to the president. Some were just angry because leaders had told them they ought to be. A few had darker motives. Really, there was no consensus on why they were there. I do know this: Rioting and feeding anger is no way forward.

Even as we condemn the offenses committed by many on January 6, we should also pause for a moment and consider from where that frustration and anger comes. It's the same anger I saw in my social media feed.

Many of the unrepeatable tweets I received came from accounts belonging to people whom I couldn't imagine would use similar language in their everyday interactions. And that told me, something was off. Why were people lashing out like this? Why were they so angry? Why were they so desperate beneath the surface? Maybe if I could understand them better, I could do something to help.

I came to the conclusion that really, at the very core, many Americans are angry because they're worried.

They worry that they're forgotten.

They worry that a growing and changing country means less opportunity for their children.

They're worried that they can't compete in a new economy where technology drives change more rapid than any we've ever experienced.

They're worried that they can't pay the bills if they get sick and they can't provide for their family like they always dreamed.

Across the land, many feel increasingly helpless or cornered.

They've earnestly turned to political leaders for hope and help—and their leaders just fed them lies and hate.

Many are flat angry because the GOP has failed to help them when it counts. Sure, they get wins in culture wars and read satisfying tweets from leaders slamming the other side. But those victories don't put food on their family table—and you can't spend tweets when you're broke. They don't think anyone cares about them.

A March 2020 poll reported 83 percent of Americans thought the then-president cared about the wealthy. Just 40 percent of respondents thought he cared about "people like me."

That's lower than both Mitt Romney and Barack Obama's number.

Alarmingly, 74 percent of independents thought the president didn't care about people like them. If independents think the leader of our party doesn't care about them, they certainly don't think the party as a whole cares about them.

I don't blame Americans for being angry with politicians on either side. I don't blame them for worrying about truly personal and consequential issues. I understand why they might feel helpless or cornered. What matters more than your child's future? Can you imagine feeling powerless to make it better? Locked into a situation you never expected and from which you feel you can't escape?

For generations, candidates have used average Americans for their votes by promising solutions to make life better—and then did not deliver. The system hasn't worked for too many people. In 2016, disenchanted voters tried a high-flying businessman and television reality star; maybe he'd be different. Maybe he'd treat them right. He gave them fulfilling rage and thrilling Twitter storms. He told them what they wanted to hear.

These Republican voters heard him say China would pay his tariffs and Mexico would pay for his wall.

They heard him say that he understood them and that he'd fight for them, not the elite.

Then these trusting Americans watched him fail to improve their healthcare. According to the New York Federal Reserve, consumers found themselves paying an extra $418 per year as his tariffs increased prices and slowed growth. American taxpayers paid for the border wall too.

And while I believe in cutting taxes wherever feasible, his 2017 tax cuts didn't help middle-class Americans nearly as much as they helped higher-income Americans.

Under the Trump tax cuts, most of the rioters on Capitol Hill paid higher tax rates than the wealthiest 400 families in the country.

People realized it. Still, our party passed the bill knowing only 29 to 33 percent of Americans approved, depending on what poll you read.

A year after the 2017 tax bill passed, only 36 percent of middle-income Americans and 28 percent of low-income Americans said the tax cuts at least helped "a little."

Do the numbers bear that out?

Well, annual GDP growth neared but didn't pass the president's 3 percent goal. Unemployment hit near-record lows before the pandemic and the stock market hit record highs during the pandemic. Middle- and lower-income Americans likely benefitted indirectly. But they didn't seem to feel it. They felt other groups benefited more.

Nor were we able to pass a bill that improved their access to affordable healthcare. The former president had that mystical grip on many middle- and lower-income voters, but when he had his chance to deliver real benefits to them, he didn't. Instead, they got scapegoats, which did nothing to put dollars in family bank accounts.

During all this time, the president and Republicans and Democrats on Capitol Hill irresponsibly let the deficit nearly double, piling up debt on American families and children. The total national debt stood at nearly $28 trillion when President Biden was inaugurated.

Remember, I now owe more than $85,000 to the U.S. Treasury as does every other American, our children included.

Our leaders in Washington weren't listening to what real people were telling them and they didn't care.

Lack of empathy cost Republicans their majorities and the White House. And we shouldn't have been surprised.

While disappointed voters had no right to storm the U.S. Capitol, citizens like them had every right to be upset. They got plenty of lip service but were ultimately forgotten yet again. In 2020, some of these disappointed voters tried Joe Biden instead—enough to win him the election.

Republicans must take time to understand those most upset by the 2020 election—especially those within our party. Let's meet them where they are and together, figure out how we can address the challenges at the root of their anger, frustration, and fear. We can level with them instead of lying to them. We can carry their burdens for a change. We can commit to understanding their deepest needs—and I guarantee you those aren't related to election fraud.

These good people don't need more disappointment or manipulation. They need—and deserve—understanding and results.

If only a minority of the country supports our policies, let's find out why. Is the policy not working or is our messaging wrong? Or do we just not understand the needs of most families? I know we want to help folks of all walks and address their worries. So how can we understand their real needs and hopes?

How can we make policy that's fair and that honors their contributions?

Let's commit to going out and just being with these fellow Republicans. "Just go love on them," as one close friend of mine would say. Then we can figure out how to help them instead of failing them.

We can help them see the promise in GOP 2.0.

If our party can learn to empathize—really get out and be with people and learn to appreciate them in a real way—both our party and our constituents will win. We can grow our tent as our policies address their needs more effectively, because we *know* their needs. Seriously, how can we expect somebody to vote for us if we're not willing to sit down with them at a kitchen table and ask them about their challenges?

How many Republican legislators know what it's like to be a single mom with two jobs and three kids?

Even after talking with Ahmaud Arbery's mother, I still don't truly comprehend what it must be like to be a young Black man in America. I never will, but I'll commit to trying.

As a party, we need to learn more about the growing Latino community. I need to sit down with more successful Asian business owners and see how our pro-growth policies can help them.

Broadly, we need to spend time with the poor, people of color, those in the middle class—many of whom don't statistically vote for us but who many of our policies could help. I don't think they're quietly grateful for the benefits we *think* or *say* trickle down to them from our economic policies and thus, we must bring our message to their dinner table. Right now, we're avoiding them and that's not working for them or us.

Building a peaceful coalition capable of winning back the White House takes welcoming voters who agree with many Republican policies, but not all.

First and tactically, we have to accept that Republicans should have healthy disagreement among themselves. It worries me that these debates have been effectively silenced in the former president's GOP. But we saw what that blind devotion to a single person's ideas and whims did to our ability to control the Big Three. A better approach is to rekindle those debates and take time to understand the stories of those with different views. Every viewpoint has a story—most likely one we don't know and have never heard because we never asked. We need to learn about one another just as much as we need to empathize with those outside our tent.

As for understanding where those outside our tent are coming from, let me tell you about a member of Georgia's congressional delegation. She's a Democrat who flipped a suburban district in 2018 and held it in 2020. She has made gun reform one of her priorities, a position that worked in her district. We don't cross paths much as she works on Capitol Hill and I work at the Georgia State Capitol, but I do respect her position because of her life experiences, even if I might disagree with a majority of her gun policies.

She lost her seventeen-year-old son, Jordan, to gun violence. Two of my sons are teenagers and I cannot fathom such a loss.

Can you imagine debating gun legislation with her and not knowing about her tragic loss? Remember "Miles's Law?" "Where you stand depends on where you sit."

Experiences and circumstances are powerful influencers, for mid-century federal bureaucrats such as Rufus Miles and for individuals of every sort. Personal situations color a person's worldview and drive people to dig in their heels. It's not right or wrong, it's just human nature. And as a party, if we don't understand those who are experiencing a different set of circumstances than we are, we'll never reach them, we won't make policy progress, and we'll certainly not win their vote. Members of our party must take time to learn. Only then can we have civil discussions that lead to worthwhile solutions.

In the state House, I represented one of the most conservative districts in the state and I knew my constituents would oppose an upcoming bill allowing the use of cannabis oil to help children with medical disorders, including seizures. Late one night, during a long session before the vote, a young page delivered a small note to me at my desk in the House chamber. It said a constituent wanted to speak with me about the medical cannabis bill. The note didn't say whether the constituent was for or against the bill. I left the chamber to hear from one of my bosses.

In the hallway, I met Kristi Baggarly. She stood there with a double stroller carrying two young girls and we began a discussion that transformed my perspective. I learned one of her daughters, Kendle, suffered from several conditions, including one causing chronic seizures. She could have up to 200 seizures in a single day. Kristi had come to lobby me on behalf of the bill. I spent an hour with her and her daughters that day, and they changed my mind.

Before, I knew only the party-line conservative perspective on the issue.

After, I understood the issue from a much better perspective: the perspective of someone who needed this treatment.

If the United States could get a man to the moon in three days, I figured surely Georgia could figure out how to make cannabis oil available to people like Kendle without opening the doors to recreational use of pot. The bill passed. Cannabis treatments significantly reduced the number of Kendle's daily seizures.

Sadly, a seizure still took her life while she slept. Kendle passed away in 2019 at age eight.

If we're honest with ourselves, many Republicans are strangers to GOP leaders. Think they don't know it? They were right to feel some leaders didn't care about their voices, struggles, and aspirations. Let's first look inward to understand those within our ranks who have differing views and experiences. How can we bear their burdens and learn to love them better? How can we engage them via our churches, charities, and communities as well as individually? Conservatives shouldn't be strangers to one another.

Then let's consider how can we look *outside* the party and take to heart the realities faced by others. I want legions of Republican burden carriers out there! Let's genuinely dig into the lives others are living. Let's understand where they're sitting. Let's *love* them.

More empathy will lead to better policy and help build the broader coalition we need to remain competitive in a changing country.

11

★ ★ ★

TONE

I'LL NEVER FORGET THE HARD BUT HONEST CONVERSATION I HAD with John Boles, the director of the Marlins' minor league system, after my first spring training with the Marlins organization. He leveled with me, it hurt, and I responded by working twice as hard because I knew what I needed to do.

Well, several seasons later, I had one of my most regretful moments in that same where-you-stand meeting. Bolsey had been promoted to manage the Florida Marlins and we had a new farm system director. I asked him for the meeting, in part because I was feeling pretty confident: "Just to continue Bolsey's tradition, let's have an honest conversation about where I stand and where I'm going."

I'd pitched two terrific seasons with back-to-back ERAs in the 2s. Truthfully, I was a little irritated that I wasn't playing in the big leagues with the Marlins in Miami, but I *clearly* deserved to be playing AAA ball.

The day of the meeting, I sat down in the office. The farm director and pitching coordinator sat down across from me.

The farm director came out and said, "It looks like you'll be in AA for a few weeks but back in AAA before you know it."

What?

I came unglued. I launched into a ten-minute tirade that I'm almost ashamed to recall or admit to. But the director never lost his composure and neither man interrupted me. They let me wear myself out. When I was finished, the director said, "Look, we're just giving you the lay of the land. The Big League roster is full, we're expecting some trades, and we just need you in AA right now. We'll get you back to where you belong soon, I promise."

I left the office, shutting the door with a little more force than I normally would. I felt great having laid into them like I did. *They deserved it for not seeing it my way.* But by the time I showered and put on my street clothes, I was flat embarrassed. I wanted to crawl inside my locker. Throughout my professional career, I prided myself on being a cool-headed practical thinker who spoke rational words in calm, confident tones. My response that day was like a normally calm person firing off an uncharacteristic 280-character rant on Twitter and then wanting to delete it an hour later. Luckily, I didn't have a Twitter account then.

Had the director and coordinator been different people, they might have spread the story and my hard-earned reputation would have evaporated in an instant. They were used to working with young men like me, however, and I like to think they realized the outburst was out of character.

Sure enough, I wound up playing AA ball in Portland, Maine. For five days. As promised, they called me up to play AAA ball in Calgary and I was back on track. A few months later, however, I tore my right shoulder, and my baseball career came to a close.

I will always regret the tone I used in that meeting. I will always appreciate the tone the director and coordinator chose for their responses. They were being empathetic, although I didn't realize it at the time. I now know that empathy is how we understand others. It's how they extended me grace when I stepped out of character because I was young, ambitious, and frustrated. Tone characterizes how we communicate with others; those two men gave me a lesson in tone I've never forgotten.

Empathy and tone are vital to the GOP's future and our party needs to improve both. Quickly.

★ ★ ★

Changing our party's tone is particularly important but uniquely difficult. Employing a better tone is playing the long game. It means having the discipline to avoid the sugar highs that come from firing off a hot 280 characters on Twitter. It's like refraining from the feels-right-in-the-moment hollering our children often deserve because we as parents know the transformative way to discipline is to talk and lead our kids to a better decision next time. I get it; good parenting is hard. Yelling can be easier.

Politics is hard too. It demands you build one type of support to get elected in the primary, another type of support to win the general, and yet another type to pass legislation. Then the next election rolls around and you have to go back and build that first kind of support again.

During all this time, you're always trying to meet fundraising goals for yourself and for the party. The more money your opponent raises, the more you need to raise to keep pace. The more the Democratic Party raises, the harder the Republican Party pushes you to raise even more. It's exhausting! How can you raise the dollars? How can you get people's attention? Then how can you get their attention again next week? It can be impossibly hard to explain policies when people want simple answers for inherently complex questions.

Many politicians begin to yell, literally and figuratively. They stop making complex arguments—it just becomes too hard and they wonder if anyone is really listening. They demonize the opposition. They cater to what their voters and funders want to hear. They make statements, posts, and videos to get media attention. They take stark policy positions to secure votes and dollars—they don't want to get primaried. Sadly, the tactics often work in terms of dollars and primary victories. But using those divisive means does not lead to a civil debate; it's been losing general elections, and it's no way to treat people or to govern.

There's a good baseball analogy here. My fastball got me drafted. A good fastball gets lots of guys drafted. As one of my first pro pitching coaches explained, however, a fastball isn't what *keeps* pitchers in the pros. Winning at that level requires something else. It takes more finesse. Winning on the mound requires a combination of many things, including velocity, location, and pitch selection. The crowd wants you to throw a fastball every pitch and blow it by the batter. They're literally yelling for you to "bring the heat!" But if you do, you'll end up losing the game. The crowd would pick a high tight fastball every time.

But the good pitcher has done his homework. He understands a batter's weaknesses. He knows what each situation calls for.

When you step up to give a speech as lieutenant governor, the crowd wants that high, tight fastball. When they see a new tweet from your account, they want that fastball. As we learned in 2020, those fastballs don't always work. Good leaders and good pitchers need exceptional visibility. They must see what's coming down the road and choose their pitches accordingly.

Too many politicians on both sides win elections and think they can keep winning with their fastball. Truth is, governing requires much more: It requires listening, studying, collaborating, compromising, explaining, and teaching.

You can do none of those things well when you're shouting your head off, and you can do none of those things when you're vilifying the very people you may need as allies on another issue. We've all but lost Ronald Reagan's idea that someone who's with you 80 percent of the time is still a friend and ally.

When you're doing none of these important things, well, there's no way you can be effective for your constituents.

In 2012, reapportionment created a new State House district in Forsyth County. My backyard was basically the boundary line, so my run started with some luck—I didn't have to move. I had never run for office but at least there was no incumbent to defeat.

Our consultant told us nothing would improve our chances more than making phone calls and knocking on doors. We rented 90 square feet of office space because it gave us access to a conference room after hours. We filled the room with volunteers at night, turning it into our own call center. When one of our callers got a policy question, somebody would wave a phone in the air, and I'd come to answer the question.

We made 6,000 calls that season. I lost count of the callers with whom I spoke.

I felt good about the conversations, whether the caller agreed with me or not. We talked about real policies and how they played out in real lives.

Today, when I'm out in Forsyth County, people still come up to me and say, "You called me during your House campaigns and answered our questions!"

I smile but rarely ask the natural next question: "Did you vote for me?"

Some pastors make a point of not knowing which church members donate the most, so they make sure they aren't tempted to love some members a little more than others. I've taken the same approach to politics. I don't want to know if you voted for me or not. You're my constituent, so I'm going to answer your questions as best I can and do my best to help you.

Besides, politics can still ruin a good conversation no matter how much love you might have in your heart.

We didn't just campaign with phone calls. Brooke, our three kids, and both sets of our parents spent months knocking on 4,000 doors in our 56,000-person district. We'd swarm a neighborhood like bees. Sometimes people weren't home; sometimes they just acted like they weren't home.

More often than you might expect, however, we'd have real conversations. My message hasn't really changed: Be honest with your words and policies. Put policy over politics. Let the people lead.

One story from that campaign truly shows the power of tone.

I'd knocked on one suburban door and I heard footsteps. An older gentleman opened the door and found an unscarred, untested, and boundlessly optimistic first-time candidate. I introduced myself and gushed about a movement I envisioned. I said, "Our state needs to put policy over politics. Elected officials need the courage to level with their constituents. They can handle the truth—their leaders just need to tell it! Beyond that, politicians shouldn't be afraid to work across the aisle if the outcome will help the people. Don't Georgians deserve better?"

He listened and said, "Would you do me a favor? Will you come in and tell that to my wife?"

Simply knocking on a door had never gotten me invited into a home before. My wife and kids were across the street and wouldn't know where'd I'd gone, but I followed him inside. He led me down a dark hallway into a darkened room where his wife lay in a hospital bed.

He said, "Honey, hear this young man. He's running for office. He's talking about honesty. I knew you'd want to know there are still honest people at the capitol."

I learned the wife was in her last days and here was this devoted husband doing his best to take care of her after she'd taken care of him for so many years. He brought her meals and anything she needed. I still get emotional thinking that he asked me in because he believed I might bring her some hope. In the bedroom, we talked about how we could make our corner of Georgia a better place for everyone's children. We talked about their hope for her future, and we talked about my hope for Georgia's future and, beyond that, my hope for politics in America. They saw the current direction and they didn't want to leave this world with America's best days in the past. I told them then, just as I'd tell you now, our best days are still to come. We are still building that shining city on the hill—we just have to start doing it a different way.

Soon this husband was in tears. His wife was in tears. I was in tears.

That conversation happened in 2012, and my optimism hasn't dimmed. It's suffered a few blows, but it's resilient.

I believe America desperately needs a better tone and the people know it.

Deep down they *want* that better tone.

It's not easy for us to turn away from the entertaining and enticing battles that play out on social media. It's fun to root for your team in what seems like a big game.

I get that. It's an easy trap for me too.

But government shouldn't be a game. Government shouldn't be reality television. Government affects real lives and real families.

The GOP should strive to lead and set a better national tone.

Nobody wins an election without speaking to more than a few Rotary Clubs, and I've lost count of the number of clubs I've visited. I always spend several days looking forward to my visits with Rotarians because I know there is zero chance of discussions drifting into partisan waters. Toward the beginning of their meetings, they recite their "Four-Way Test." I can't think of a better guide to governing our political tone.

Rotarians evaluate their statements by asking:

1. Is it the truth?
2. Is it fair to all concerned?
3. Will it build goodwill and better friendships?
4. Will it be beneficial to all concerned?

It seemed a bit simple when I first heard it. As I kept hearing it in club after club, however, I began to see its wisdom. I'd listen to CEOs of Georgia's largest companies and leaders of our largest organizations stand up and repeat the Four-Way Test before lunch, and it left an impression on me.

I'm sure every statement made by every Rotarian doesn't meet the test, but nobody expects perfection, right? Even our Constitution refers to a "more perfect Union," not a "perfect Union." We're all on a journey and doing our best is the most we can expect of one another. Good on Rotarians for trying.

Rotarians themselves didn't create the test. It came from a business executive trying to save an aluminum company during the 1930s. The company was nearly bankrupt both in the financial and cultural sense. Club Aluminum was $400,000 in debt and Herbert Taylor knew he couldn't fix the financial situation without first addressing the ethical one.

He came up with the Four-Way Test and made it the standard throughout his company. He decided every leader must model the four tests in all their actions and see that it cascaded to all 250 employees. If it didn't, Taylor worried the Club Aluminum Company would collapse along with so many other Depression-era businesses. Because of his leadership, however, Club veered away from bankruptcy and began to thrive even as Taylor applied the Four-Way Test to his advertising and sales department! His company would practice truth-in-advertising. They wouldn't push a customer into a bad deal just to meet sales goals. The company also stopped treating or discussing competitors in negative ways. The test transformed the culture and saved the company along with 250 jobs. Club Aluminum paid off its debt in five years and grew profitable once again.

Taylor, who served as president of the Chicago Rotary Club, must have had confidence in his product and service. If he hadn't, he might have seen misleading advertising and unfair sales practices as necessary to keep the business going. But he knew his company could compete without taking shortcuts. He knew proud and valued employees would perform better than those in a culture that lacked fairness and honesty.

I feel about the GOP the same way Taylor felt about his company. If conservative policies were inferior, I'd understand the tone many leaders use today. But our policies are *not* inferior! Every bit of me believes our policies are *better* for people than the opposition's. The Republican Party should not need divisive and rancorous tone to advance its agenda. GOP 2.0 certainly doesn't.

If we stick to conservative policy, take time to understand voters' real needs, and set an example of serving others, our new movement will win elections for the party once again.

★ ★ ★

Friends, the PET Project goes nowhere without honesty.

And the GOP goes nowhere good without honesty.

Winning back the public's trust must be Priority One.

To me, GOP 2.0 should lead us to a place where when Republicans walk into a room, we'll be taken seriously again. When we say something, people should be able to take it to the bank. We should be known as the adults in the room who shoot straight. People should know they'll hear the truth from us, whether they want to hear it or not—and whether we want to tell it or not.

Intellectual honestly is a starting point. It's the sum total of the PET Project. If you want to get the policy right, you need good data. If you're truly being empathic, you're leveling with another person and hearing his or her perspective—and I hope you're using a common set of facts. And if you're concerned about tone, you're listening more than shouting and making an argument responsibly and respecting the other person by being truthful.

I believe elected, appointed, and hired officials should do their homework to design the best policies possible. Having worked on major policy initiatives such as healthcare and education, I know data matters in development, implementation, and evaluation. If we're not intellectually honest when developing policies, the policies won't work. Politicians might win the political point and raise some dollars by leaning on misinformation, but they'll eventually lose when voters realize their policies are disasters.

When I walk into a room full of Democrats, they know I'll be intellectually honest with them. I have positional authority in that room as president of the senate, but nobody will give me the time of day unless I have moral authority. I think I've come to a place where our Democratic senators may not always agree with me, but they'll hear me out.

I've been a businessman much longer than I've been a politician, so that's the lens I look through when I'm trying to solve a problem. I'll invite you to ask yourself these questions:

- "What business would tolerate individuals lying or spreading misinformation?"
- "What business would develop policy based on bad data?"

- "What successful company designs strategy without trying to understand the needs of all stakeholders?"
- "What executive gets to yell at employees and vilify customers?"

None, right? As Republicans, we need to operate in our political conversations the same way we do in our professional conversations—and in our faith conversations!

Non-elected citizens have the luxury of indulging fantasies, but those responsible for governing do not. The party of Lincoln should not dissemble. Let's ground our words and decisions in data so our policies will ultimately succeed.

I teach my three boys the importance of truth every day; how can we make the party an example for our children once again?

Like many other parents, Brooke and I teach our kids that "Honesty is the best policy."

I may not have fully believed the maxim when I first heard it as a kid, but I sure believe it now. It's become the law at the Duncan household and in the Georgia Senate.

And it should be the law in the Grand Old Party too.

Honesty should guide discussions among party members and with others. Dishonesty in 2020 cost the GOP the White House and Senate. Voters didn't trust the president—and with some reason. *The Washington Post* tagged him with 30,573 false or misleading claims during his term. And our party leaders tolerated and even supported his behavior, which went far beyond simply putting partisan spin on an issue. Lie by lie, the former president sapped the trustworthiness of every single Republican official.

Misinformation suppressed Republican turnout in Georgia's 2021 senate runoffs. If the party had tried honesty in the months after the 2020 election, Republicans would still hold the U.S. Senate and have real influence in Washington.

Further, a February 2021 Gallup poll found the Republican Party's national favorability numbers fell to 36 percent, down from 43 percent in November. Did folks who wouldn't vote Republican anyway drive the drop? Nope. They already had a low opinion. The drop came from voters identifying as Republican. Their favorable opinion of their own party dropped twelve points from 90 percent to 78 percent.

I guarantee misinformation was a driver.

Republican leaders have excused, accepted, encouraged, and rewarded making false statements on an astonishing scale recently, especially for a party that claims moral high ground. Leaders are misleading members into sharing misinformation with children and showing them dishonesty doesn't have consequences, as long as the fibbers are part of your own tribe. We rail about schools damaging children by not teaching traditional history in classrooms. We bemoan the lack of values in public school. Then we stand by quietly when fellow party members are teaching kids dishonesty and lack-of-consequence in real life?

What's conservative about that?

What's *American* about that?

In a party very concerned about what liberal ideas public schools might teach our children, it seems odd that our party's leaders stand by and let character education go out the window.

Officials are also using bad information to make decisions. A republic cannot function without an honestly informed populace and a dialogue based in truth. This rampant lying and tolerance for untruth have to stop. Otherwise, it's like we're simultaneously rotting and battering the foundation of Ronald Reagan's famous shining city on a hill.

Consider just the most recent fruits of Republican-spread misinformation: election losses, a riot at the U.S. Capitol, a second impeachment, an election reform spectacle.

I don't know about you, but I'm tired of this path.

Rampant misinformation has also created a dangerous erosion of trust. Few Republicans find almost any traditional news outlets credible. *The Wall Street Journal* and Fox News register as barely credible in GOP eyes; everyone else is very biased at best, sinisterly fake at worst. In fall 2020, 89 percent of Republicans didn't trust mass media to report news fairly or accurately. I'm not afraid to call out media bias—and there is *plenty*—but when we think media is biased because they don't report what we *want* to hear or they don't echo the falsehoods our leaders perpetuate, that's a problem. And it's a problem when leaders completely undermine trust in a vital democratic institution like our free press.

Conservative leaders and pundits railed against the media for reporting there was no election fraud in Georgia. While major outlets *are* often biased against conservatives and frequently *do* deserve the railing-against, ABC, CBS, CNN, NBC, PBS—and *The New York Times*, *The Wall Street Journal*, and countless others on the print side—seemed to call it straight on election fraud.

Particularly from where I was sitting in Georgia, the mainstream media was telling the truth, at least on the issue of fraud.

Yes, there was bias; there always is. But here, the media reported the core issue accurately: *There wasn't rampant fraud.*

Many of the outlets most trusted by conservatives did *not* report the core facts accurately, and they now face very substantial legal peril for knowingly reporting false information. They discarded journalistic integrity, chased ratings and dollars, and forgot their obligation to inform the citizens of our republic.

They gave airtime to conspiracy theories that baselessly attacked Dominion Systems and Smartmatic among others. When those companies announced lawsuits in December 2020, outlets such as Fox News and Newsmax immediately took defensive action. Fox News filmed an interview with election technology expert Eddie Perez who debunked the most common fraud allegations in short order. Fox ran the interview on shows whose hosts and guests had most aggressively pushed conspiracy theories, especially those involving Dominion and Smartmatic.

For its part, Newsmax quickly posted a telling disclaimer on its website and read it on air:

> Since election day, various guests, attorneys and elected officials have appeared on Newsmax TV and offered opinions and claims about Smartmatic and Dominion Systems, both companies that offer voting software in the U.S.
>
> Newsmax would like to clarify its news coverage and note it has not reported as true certain claims made about these companies.
>
> There are several facts our viewers and readers should be aware. Newsmax has found no evidence either Dominion or Smartmatic owns the other, or has any business association with each other.

We have no evidence Dominion uses Smartmatic's software or vice versa.

No evidence has been offered that Dominion or Smartmatic used software or reprogrammed software that manipulated votes in the 2020 election.

Smartmatic has stated its software was only used in the 2020 election in Los Angeles, and was not used in any battleground state contested by the Trump campaign and Newsmax has no evidence to the contrary.

Dominion has stated its company has no ownership relationship with the House Speaker Nancy Pelosi's family, Sen. Dianne Feinstein's family, the Clinton family, Hugo Chavez, or the government of Venezuela.

Neither Dominion nor Smartmatic has any relationship with George Soros.

Smartmatic is a U.S. company and not owned by the Venezuelan government, Hugo Chavez or any foreign official or entity.

Smartmatic states it has no operations in Venezuela. While the company did election projects in Venezuela from 2004 to 2017, it states it never was founded by Hugo Chavez, nor did it have a corrupt relationship with him or the Venezuelan government.

It was all fun and games and ratings bonanzas for these networks until they realized the law might hold them to account. When push came to shove, they had to admit nobody had any evidence of anything.

The astounding volume of post-election misinformation simply overwhelmed the outlets that were trying to tell the straight story. Unfortunately, the outlets now in legal jeopardy for spreading misinformation were the ones to which many Republicans listened. Conservative citizens *trusted* these news outlets, and the outlets irresponsibly misled them so they could get better ratings. These outlets weren't biased against Republicans, but they were downright unscrupulous and manipulative.

Consequently, at the end of January 2021, just 32 percent percent of Republicans considered the 2020 election free and fair. At the same time, 98 percent of Democrats and 73 percent of independents thought Joe Biden had rightfully won the presidency.

Here's something else lies have accomplished: The 2020 election results made 53 percent of Democrats more motivated to vote in 2022, but only 36 percent of Republicans felt the same. We've de-motivated our party with fraud fantasies. Our members have started thinking their votes don't matter because Republican leaders have told them the system is rigged.

The fires of misinformation have convinced four in ten Republicans they're getting a raw deal. They think using violence is now an acceptable option "if elected leaders won't protect America;" 55 percent support using force to protect traditional American values. Nearly 30 percent of Republicans believe false theories about the president battling a deep-state ring of child sex traffickers. Half of Republicans believe antifa was behind the Capitol riots (it wasn't). Conservative leaders and conservative media primed the pump for fringe groups to exert dangerous influence like this.

One last fruit of misinformation comes in the fact that at the time of this writing, only 39 percent of Republicans were planning to get the COVID-19 vaccine. The former president boasted about Operation Warp Speed producing three vaccines but never aggressively pushed Americans to get vaccinated. In part, he didn't want to alienate the Republican anti-vaccination faction. His one comment encouraging Americans to get the vaccine at February 2021's CPAC meeting made news because it was so rare.

Let me tell you: Independent swing voters are watching this circus and walking away.

But you know who's still buying tickets? Foreign governments like Russia.

They see a party flooding its own people with misinformation and priming them not to believe any traditional news sources. This enables foreign actors to stage misinformation campaigns that their targets embrace without a second thought. Misled Republicans following the former president and conspiracy-minded GOP leaders will embraces these lies and further enable the Kremlin's efforts to influence politics in the United States of America.

Let me tell you this too. At the height of the Fraud Hoax, when it seemed the entire party had turned on me, I learned the Georgia Bureau of Investigation had found a website with my image—and that of the governor—with my face centered in crosshairs. The site had our personal information, too, including our addresses and pictures of our homes. The GBI and FBI briefed us several weeks later that the people behind the website were Iranian terrorists trying to destabilize our country.

Misinformation is a dangerous national security issue, and it makes our country vulnerable. The leaders who are spreading misinformation and misplaced hatred or letting it spread are doing Iran's work and irresponsibly threatening our national security.

They need to stop it. Now.

★ ★ ★

GOP 2.0's leaders will meet people where they are today and help them assess their information channels. Nobody is changing their mind about fraud and the president's character overnight. And I'm not holding anyone's view against them, given the forces that have besieged the party. I do hope, going forward, we can work together to turn down the volume on irresponsible ringleaders and help citizens once again make their own decisions based on facts. Let's stop undermining every information channel that doesn't always see it our way. Let's call out falsehood. Let's promote policies that don't need misinformation to win support.

We need institutional help too. Churches, Charities, and Corporations need to call out misinformation and hold politicians accountable, like they hold their officers and employees accountable. Citizens too. In all our circles, we must speak up when others spread rumors that undermine our nation's future.

As a lieutenant governor who oversaw a fair election that gave Georgia to Joe Biden, I was on the receiving end of these conspiracy theories. I can tell you they're not true, as much as believers may want them to be. I saw the real damage they caused. I know they hurt the people who believe them, and I know they could destroy our national fabric and our democracy itself.

Misinformation breeds mistrust.

Falsehood undermines freedom.

This does not end well.

Now, some of you are thinking, "Democrats' noses can grow just as long as Republicans' can! They spread misinformation too!"

Yes, they do! You're 100 percent right. The other side needs a lesson in honesty.

That doesn't matter though. Republicans have to govern ourselves because, frankly, we can't govern them. What we *can* do is let our actions speak loudly. We can show America our values and win back their trust and their vote. We should avoid the rampant what-about-ism that infects our nation. We can't excuse our own bad behavior because someone else—"they"—did it first.

The Duncan kids tried that back in kindergarten. It didn't work for them then, it doesn't work for them now, and it shouldn't work for the fully grown adult leaders in the Republican Party.

EPILOGUE

★ ★ ★

THE BALLFIELD
IN THE SHINING CITY

"I've spoken of the shining city all my political life, but I don't know if I ever quite communicated what I saw when I said it. But in my mind it was a tall, proud city built on rocks stronger than oceans, wind-swept, God-blessed, and teeming with people of all kinds living in harmony and peace; a city with free ports that hummed with commerce and creativity. And if there had to be city walls, the walls had doors and the doors were open to anyone with the will and the heart to get here. That's how I saw it, and see it still."

—Ronald Reagan,
farewell address to the nation,
January 11, 1989

PRESIDENT REAGAN SPOKE OF HIS "SHINING CITY" TIME AND again during his eight years in office. The optimistic vision he shared earned him a 17-million-vote victory in 1984 and restored Americans' confidence in ourselves and our nation.

His vision resurrected the conservative cause. It defined generations of citizens.

Despite the modern storms battering it, our American citadel sits today on firmer ground than any other. No competing nation has such spirit and still-unbounded potential. The winds blowing from the left and right are testing our walls, and the gusts won't subside soon. But I'm confident our nearly 250-year-old city will prove resilient yet again.

Ronald Reagan elevated that hilltop image to embody our nation's very freedom, leadership, and prosperity. America as Reagan saw it—as that beautiful shining city—was a beacon to the world, summoning other peoples and nations to realize their aspirations just as we were realizing ours. The power of Reagan's imagery comes from every American's ability to imagine that city for themselves. No one vision is right or wrong, or better or worse than another. What's important is our ability to believe together in America's destiny and to know our fates are all intertwined.

★ ★ ★

When I think about the shining city on the hill, I'm pretty convinced there's a ballfield smack in the middle.

I don't envision the ballfield just because I played baseball years ago. I envision it because it represents so much of America as I see it. We may speak of great national ideas and movements, but at the end the day, local actions and communities sustain this country. And those communities have been continually built, tested, and rebuilt on ballfields in almost every town in this land.

You can sense the magic of America on warm summer evenings when fireflies part ways for fastballs. You can see citizenship's roots when locals pitch in to fix up the field or when players learn to win and lose. Understanding begins when cheers in English are just as loud as ones in Spanish, when coaches with darker skin teach players with lighter skin, when moms and dads coach sons and daughters.

My view of America started to form on baseball diamonds in the seven states my family called home. Minor league ballfields in countless small towns and the guys with whom I played both strengthened and tempered my views. Being a husband, father, coach, entrepreneur, and elected official all shaped my perspectives in unique ways that I wouldn't change for the world. All these experiences have led me to envision the America I want for my boys, just as I'm sure your own experiences lead you to imagine the type of country you want your own children to inherit.

You don't need to be a baseball fan to follow me here. My middle son Bayler loves stepping up to home plate with a bat in his hand. My youngest son Ryder will cheer him on but would rather be on a studio sound stage, script in hand. If Ryder imagined the shining city, he'd see a theatre in its center.

Everyone can envision a place where families fill the seats or sidelines, where people clap for runs and goals, beauty, and effort. We can all imagine a place where commerce is brisk—lines form for tickets, merch, hot dogs, and drinks. People enjoy one another's company in peace and security, safe from any who might do them harm. They share a mutual love for competition or performance or community. They root for the underdogs. They come together at their community's heart.

That's how I see America.

And *together* is how I envision GOP 2.0 making America greater than ever before.

Our movement will summon an extraordinary coalition of loving people who build one another up and who believe in that singularly powerful and unifying American ideal: freedom. Our movement will fortify that shining city, however we might imagine it. We'll sweep away the debris left by the recent past and polish the flagpoles. We'll open the doors wide.

Freedom's holy light will shine brighter from our rooftops, and the world will notice.

★ ★ ★

Underdogs are by nature optimists. We are dreamers too. And I believe in the power of dreaming together.

So I won't be discouraged by those who say our task is impossible—that the Republican Party has gone round the bend and can never return to principles for which it used to stand. I refuse to believe the party once led by Lincoln and Reagan, Teddy Roosevelt and Eisenhower, has forsaken truth and democracy for power and a despot.

I've heard many quiet voices who seek a better way forward, a reasoned conservative direction that will strengthen and unify our nation rather than weaken and divide it. These earnest voices want a path marked by the values they teach their children: honesty, kindness, responsibility.

I am not dreaming alone. I'm dreaming together with that great silenced majority, and we are speaking up and taking back America's conservative party. We're ready for a party of which we can be proud again, leaders we can trust again, brave examples that we can once again point out to our children.

We imagine a government of representatives who vigorously and honestly debate big ideas and then come together to take responsibility for helping our nation solve its challenges. We envision leaders who act like adults, who make the tough choices, tell the hard truths, and learn from the hard lessons. We envision leaders who can show us how to love one another, even when we disagree. We want a party that cares about making Americans great rather than a party that just aims to elevate one American in particular.

Ultimately, we all want to see an America where everyone has the freedom to thrive.

These simple, decent hopes will build our city.

These dreams will rally our coalition.

These aspirations define GOP 2.0.

I'm daring enough to dream big, but practical enough to stay grounded. And even if I weren't that practical, daily newsfeeds from Washington would keep my feet on the ground. Our country faces severe challenges. It's a tough landscape for truth, reason, and civility. It's a daunting proposition to take on history's wealthiest, loudest, and most powerful political machine. I realize we dreamers have a difficult path. I see the polls that show unflinching support for the former president's leadership.

Those who see beyond him know we're not the ones off course. I am entirely convinced we are on the right path. We are doing the right thing by standing up for truth and decency.

As I shared with Bayler years ago at that campfire, "Doing the right thing will never be the wrong thing."

It's scary taking the path less traveled. It rattles you when a vast majority seem set against your ideas—especially when they seem unwaveringly bent on pleasing an ex-president whose time has passed.

It rattles you even more when you've been sharing your vision with anyone who will listen, and many people still don't hear you. Well, I've been unheard before. I've been written off and I've had near-zero name recognition. Yet I've fought for a better vision, I've taken on the party's political machine, and I've won statewide. I know the power of good ideas and how they can swell into a powerful current that brings real change to people in need.

I believe in GOP 2.0 with all my heart and those opposing us should be forewarned: I am digging in and fighting for my party's soul and our country's future.

I'm asking you to fight right alongside me because conservative principles and American values are too important for us to give in.

Friends, we are playing the long game, but we have the perseverance for it. The coming months and years will see Republicans wake up, one-by-one. They'll realize they've been misled, and we'll welcome them into GOP 2.0. We are on the right side of history. And in the end, we will win.

★ ★ ★

Five o'clock is my usual time to wake up. I'm a happy early riser and when my eyes open, I can't wait for my feet to hit the ground. While no two days are exactly alike, each one begins with a walk to the kitchen for a cup of coffee. I spend thirty minutes (or more if I have time) reading a devotional and spending time alone in that rare early morning quiet. It gives you time to remember who you are and whose you are. You can remind yourself of your most important goals and why it's so vital that you reach them.

For me, that predawn peace reminds me I'm a baseball player turned businessman who stumbled into politics. You've heard the expression "playing with house money," right? In Las Vegas, that means you're gambling with money that's not really yours anyway, so why not roll the dice? If you win, you can hit a jackpot. If you lose, you lose. You're not out any real cash and you'll never wonder "what if I'd gone big?"

I often say I'm playing with house money.

I never expected to be lieutenant governor—I gambled big and won. If I gamble big again and lose, that's okay. My dreams have never been about political office. That frees me up to speak my mind and stand for what I believe, even when it draws fire. These past months have thickened my skin even more; I can take the hits that will come. And I'm still excited to go to work on conservative policies that I believe help real people and share a message I truly believe in and that I want my family to believe in too.

That precious morning time reminds me I'm not my own person.

I belong to Brooke Duncan, who has been my partner in life since we were both teenagers. She has never left my side and I would never leave hers. Three young men own equal shares of me too. Every day is a new challenge for me to do right by them, be an example, and make them proud.

Eleven million Georgians are also Duncan shareholders. The decisions I make under Georgia's Gold Dome are to help them as best I can. On any decision I make, some of my constituents will disagree with me. Sometimes a few, sometimes a lot. It can be tough knowing that. What I tell them is this: I will always, *always* do what I think is right in the long-term for Georgians. I promise to put *their* future first, *their* families first.

I'm honored to serve them as lieutenant governor, and I'm equally honored to serve those who voted for me as I am to serve those who didn't.

Above all, I belong to my Lord. I read His words and work really, really hard to live up to His expectations and the example of Jesus. Understanding, love, and forgiveness—Jesus's great lessons—are traits I consistently fail to live by. But that's not because I don't try. Like most of us, I need to try harder. If we can all seek to live out those three words in our real lives and interactions with others, I know our nation and party will find a better course. We can heal one another. We can restore the pervasive spirit of optimism and shared citizenship that has always marked America.

And if—*if*—the Republican Party can shake off its loyalty to wronghearted leaders, and if our party can understand, love, and forgive others, I believe we can find a better way forward and elect a new kind of Republican president in 2024.

I'm *convinced* this generation of Republicans and this refreshed and bigger version of the party I imagine—GOP 2.0—can bring together an extraordinary coalition behind conservative policies that work, genuine understanding that informs, and respectful honest tones that unite and inspire.

Dream with me.

Imagine how we'll feel when we watch a proud Republican leading *all* Americans in celebrating our nation's 250th birthday on July 4, 2026. Appropriately, a conservative president will honor our Founders and those brave minutemen, farmers, and misfits who had the audacity to pick a fight with the world's largest empire. Nobody thought they'd win, except themselves—and that's all that mattered.

My fellow Americans, my fellow Republicans, let's put the past behind us and meet together under GOP 2.0's big tent to seek a better way forward for this party and this country. Let's forge a better future for our families and for all families. Let's restore our belief in ourselves and with love in our hearts and optimism in our step, let's get to work.

We have a House, Senate, and White House to reclaim.

ACKNOWLEDGMENTS

In the book's conclusion, I wrote that I'm not entirely my own person—and this isn't entirely my own book. So many people have contributed to make *GOP 2.0* possible as well as make my own story possible. From baseball coaches and teammates in more cities and towns than I can count to those steadfast supporters who believed a former baseball player-turned-businessman might have something to offer the state of Georgia, a Godsent cast of people have shaped my journey and, in many ways, made it possible. I am humbled and grateful, and I'll give highest credit straight to the Lord.

Without the best political volunteers and believers in the world, an underdog like me would never have walked into the Georgia State Capitol. You got me here and I won't let you down. Today I have a terrific team who, along with me, make up the Office of the Lieutenant Governor. I'm proud of what we've achieved together to date. Your hard work has made our state better—and we're by no means done making progress. A sincere thanks goes to my dedicated colleagues on both sides of the aisle in the General Assembly and especially to our state senators. I've been honored to serve alongside Governor Brian Kemp, who, like me, has Georgia's finest law enforcement officers by his side. Devoted Georgia State Troopers have taken exceptional care of me and logged long hours on watch, especially during the thick of the 2020 election fallout. My respect for them grows daily. And during those trying post-election weeks, so many good people from across the country reached out to let me know I wasn't alone. My family's wonderful church community, small group, and pastor also walked alongside us. Your kindness and reassurance meant more than you'll ever know.

A special thank you goes to my Dream Team who believed in this project and GOP 2.0 early on and who supported and encouraged me to pursue big ideas even when the winds were definitely not at our backs. Our publisher, Jonathan Merkh, was enthusiastic about this book from the outset, and our editor, Mitchell Ivers, guided it across the finish line. Their help was very appreciated by this first-time author.

At home, our three boys are the center of our universe. Brooke and I couldn't imagine life without them. We've both learned more from them than we could ever teach them. I am lucky and grateful. Our boys are in turn lucky to have four grandparents who love on them at every opportunity and show them what faith and love look like. And what can I say to my wife, Brooke? You changed my life years ago and still make it better each day. We will always be in this together and I can't wait to see where God leads us next.

To those of you who read this book, I appreciate your time and hope parts of my message resonated with you. The GOP 2.0 movement is an audacious project but one I believe will usher in a new era for America's conservative party and for the country itself. I'll certainly acknowledge here that I don't have all the answers or ideas and I'll need your help. I hope you'll reach out, visit GOP2.org, and join me on this new journey.

REFERENCES

INTRODUCTION: GOP 2.0

24   "Those joining the GOP 2.0 movement": Noemie Emery, "Tea Party Conservatives Should Seek out More of Reagan's '80-Percent Friends'," *Washington Examiner*, October 22, 2013, www.washingtonexaminer.com/tea-party-conservatives-should-seek-out-more-of-reagans-80-percent-friends.

24   "To add bipartisan diversity": Joe Klein, "If You Agree with Me on 9 Out of 12 Issues," TIME.com, , September 22, 2014, time.com/3419078/if-you-agree-with-me-on-9-out-of-12-issues/.

1: NOVEMBER: THE FRAUD HOAX

32   "The county's demographics were also changing": "Quick Facts: Forsyth County, Georgia," United States Census Bureau/U.S. Department of Commerce, accessed May 19, 2021, www.census.gov/quickfacts/forsythcountygeorgia.

32   "In the 2020 election, conservative stalwart": Mitchell Thorson, Janie Haseman, and Carlie Procell, "Four Maps That Show How America Voted in the 2020 Election with Results by County, Number of Voters," *USA Today*, November 10, 2020, www.usatoday.com/in-depth/graphics/2020/11/10/election-maps-2020-america-county-results-more-voters/6226197002/.

32   "Another suburban Atlanta county, Henry": Tamar Hallerman, "How Changes in Henry, Rockdale Helped Biden Capture Georgia," *Atlanta Journal-Constitution*, December 30, 2020, www.ajc.com/politics/how-changes-in-henry-rockdale-helped-biden-capture-georgia/LBT7R6QIXNEEPLFD2TMLTOC2W4/.

34   "Prior to the pandemic, Colorado": Olivia B. Waxman, "Voting by Mail Dates Back to America's Earliest Years. Here's How It's Changed Over the Years," TIME.com, September 28, 2020, time.com/5892357/voting-by-mail-history/.

34   "Thus a great body of evidence": Daniel M. Thompson et al., *Universal Vote-by-Mail Has No Impact on Partisan Turnout or Vote Share*, Democracy

& Polarization Lab, Stanford University, May 6, 2020, www.andrewbenja-minhall.com/Thompson_et_al_VBM.pdf.

34 "The conservative Heritage Foundation": "A Sampling of Recent Election Fraud Cases from Across the United States," The Heritage Foundation, accessed May 19, 2021, www.heritage.org/voterfraud.

63 "Through dogged repetition": "60% View Joe Biden's 2020 Presidential Victory As Legitimate, Quinnipiac University National Poll Finds; 77% Of Republicans Believe There Was Widespread Voter Fraud," Quinnipiac University, December 10, 2020, poll.qu.edu/poll-release?releaseid=3734.

75 "A twenty-something employee of Dominion": Ali Swenson, "Video Doesn't Show an Election Tech Manipulating Votes in Georgia," Associated Press, December 2, 2020, apnews.com/article/fact-checking-9771056788.

3: JANUARY: TWO RUNOFFS AND A RANSACKING

78 "Secretary of State Brad Raffensperger picked up the line": Paulina Firozi, and Amy Gardner, "Here's the Full Transcript and Audio of the Call between Trump and Raffensperger," *Washington Post*, January 5, 2021, www.washingtonpost.com/politics/trump-raffensperger-call-transcript-georgia-vote/2021/01/03/2768e0cc-4ddd-11eb-83e3-322644d82356_story.html.

85 Stracqualursi, Veronica. "Trump's Chief of Staff Mark Meadows Pushed DOJ to Investigate Baseless Election Fraud Claims." *FOX Carolina*, 5 June 2021, www.foxcarolina.com/news/politics/trumps-chief-of-staff-mark-meadows-pushed-doj-to-investigate-baseless-election-fraud-claims/article_fa505336-679e-57a3-a9d3-7742b9793243.html.

85 "That led to a contentious White House meeting": Katie Benner, "Trump and Justice Dept. Lawyer Said to Have Plotted to Oust Acting Attorney General," *New York Times*, January 22, 2021, www.nytimes.com/2021/01/22/us/politics/jeffrey-clark-trump-justice-department-election.html?searchResultPosition=1.

91 "All eyes fell on Georgia": Chris Joyner, "The Results Are in: Georgia Senate Races Shatter Donation, Spending Records," *Chattanooga Times Free Press*, February 6, 2021, www.timesfreepress.com/news/break-ingnews/story/2021/feb/06/results-are-ga-senate-races-shatter-dona-tion-spending-records/541084/?bcsubid=8642ecc2-8f09-4c86-ac6b-7e967da5d707&pbdialog=reg-wall-login-created-tfp.

93 "The president's PAC": Adam Brewster, "Trump's New PAC Raises over $30 Million," CBS News, February 2, 2021, www.cbsnews.com/news/save-america-trump-pac-raises-30-million/; Zach Montellaro

and Elena Schneider, "Trump's Post-Election Cash Grab Floods Funds to New PAC," Politico.com, December 4, 2020, www.politico.com/news/2020/12/03/trump-pac-fundraising-442775.

93   "At last reporting": Chris Riotta, "Trump Raised over $200 Million after Election Day. Just $8.8 Million Has Gone towards Challenging the Vote," *The Independent*, December 4, 2020, www.independent.co.uk/news/world/americas/us-politics/trump-legal-effort-fundraising-recount-election-2024-b1766547.html.

94   "Nearly half thought": "Biden Begins Presidency with Positive Ratings; Trump Departs with Lowest-Ever Job Mark," U.S. Politics & Policy, Pew Research Center, January 15, 2021, www.pewresearch.org/politics/2021/01/15/biden-begins-presidency-with-positive-ratings-trump-departs-with-lowest-ever-job-mark/.

95   "Both of Georgia's then-U.S. Senators": Jason Lemon, "Georgia GOP Senators Back Texas AG's Lawsuit to Overturn Their Own State's Election." *Newsweek*, December 8, 2020, www.newsweek.com/georgia-gop-senators-back-texas-ags-lawsuit-overturn-their-own-states-election-1553321; Tia Mitchell and Maya T. Prabhu, "Georgia Republican Lawmakers Say They Were Right to Back Texas Lawsuit against State," *Atlanta Journal-Constitution*, December 21, 2020, www.ajc.com/politics/georgia-republican-lawmakers-say-they-were-right-to-back-texas-lawsuit-against-state/KNYRTPJUAJHMBGWXQKVE43AQMY/.

95   "Seven Republican Senators": Barbara Sprunt, "Here Are the Republicans Who Objected to the Electoral College Count," NPR.org, January 7, 2021, www.npr.org/sections/insurrection-at-the-capitol/2021/01/07/954380156/here-are-the-republicans-who-objected-to-the-electoral-college-count.

98   "Let me add a warning": Stephen Elliott, "Bar Associations Criticize Lyle Resolution." *Nashville Post*, March 2, 2021, www.nashvillepost.com/courts/bar-associations-criticize-lyle-resolution/article_91326cfe-c014-5171-85c1-d8991bc407b9.html.

101   "It's worth noting a close associate": Roger Sollenberger, "Six Degrees of Sedition: Was Master Trickster Roger Stone behind Capitol Riot?," Salon.com, January 29, 2021, www.salon.com/2021/01/29/six-degrees-of-sedition-was-master-trickster-roger-stone-behind-the-capitol-riot/.

4: FEBRUARY-APRIL: CHAOS CONTINUES

111   "You know I like data points": Tony Fabrizio and David Lee, "Memorandum: American Voters Want Choices to Safely Cast Ballots,"

Fabrizio Lee National Poll Memo, April 29, 2020, www.documentcloud. org/documents/6880238-Fabrizio-Lee-National-Poll-Memo.html.

111 "And I'll add that Republicans": Stephen Fowler and David Armstrong, "16 Years Later, Georgia Lawmakers Flip Views on Absentee Voting," Georgia Public Broadcasting, March 7, 2021, www.gpb.org/ news/2021/03/07/16-years-later-georgia-lawmakers-flip-views-on-absentee-voting.

111 "One more fact made repealing": Kevin Kosar , Marc Hyden, and Steven Greenhut, "The Conservative Case for Expanded Access to Absentee Ballots," R Street, June 2020, www.rstreet.org/wp-content/ uploads/2020/06/Short-No.-90-Expanded-Access-to-Absentee-Ballots. pdf.

117 "The narrative pumped out by the left": Quinn Scanlan, "Breaking down Claims about Georgia's Election Law: What's True and What's Not?" ABC News, April 7, 2021, abcnews.go.com/Politics/ breaking-claims-georgias-election-law-true/story?id=76897349.

119 "I'd left people on both sides of the aisle": Greg Bluestein, "Duncan Not Expected to Run for Reelection as Georgia's No. 2, His Aide Says," *Atlanta Journal-Constitution*, April 8, 2021, www.ajc.com/politics/politics-blog/duncan-not-expected-to-run-for-re-election-as-georgias-no-2/ Y2LCK2QWIRGDJNKMHQNLFNSKGY/.

121 "I thought Georgia journalist Jay Bookman": Jay Bookman, "Bookman: Recalling Zell While Geoff Duncan Risks 'Doing the Right Thing,'" *Georgia Recorder*, March 18, 2021, georgiarecorder.com/2021/03/18/ bookman-recalling-zell-while-geoff-duncan-risks-doing-the-right-thing/.

5: PIVOT POINT

136 "As far as I'm concerned, everything is great": David Siders, "'Everything's Great': GOP Ditches Election Post-Mortems," Politico. com, December 17, 2020, www.politico.com/news/2020/12/17/ gop-ditches-election-postmortem-447091.

142 "A Gallup poll released in February": Jeffrey M. Jones, "GOP Image Slides Giving Democrats Strong Advantage," Gallup.com, February 10, 2021, news.gallup.com/poll/329561/gop-image-slides-giving-democrats-strong-advantage.aspx.

143 "The president's approval": Isa Alomran and Ethan Winter "Trump's Approval Rating Dropping Among Independents, Republicans," Data for Progress, January 13, 2021, www.dataforprogress.org/blog/2021/1/13/ trumps-approval-rating-dropping-among-independents-republicans.

144 "The first weeks of 2021": Dante Chinni, "GOP Registration

Drop after Capitol Attack Is Part of Larger Trend," NBC News, February 7, 2021, www.msn.com/en-us/news/politics/gop-reg-istration-drop-after-capitol-attack-is-part-of-larger-trend/ar-BB1dtjKA?ocid=msedgntp.

144 "Eight thousand left the party in North Carolina": Dante Chinni, "GOP Registration Drop after Capitol Attack Is Part of Larger Trend," NBC News, February 7, 2021, www.msn.com/en-us/news/politics/gop-registration-drop-after-capitol-attack-is-part-of-larger-trend/ar-BB1dtjKA?ocid=msedgntp.

144 "In the week after the riots": Ben Christopher, "California Republican Party Lost Over 33,000 Members After U.S. Capitol Stormed," *Times of San Diego*, February 7, 2021, timesofsandiego.com/politics/2021/02/07/california-republican-party-lost-over-33000-members-after-u-s-capitol-stormed/.

144 "In Colorado, 4,600 Republicans": Reid Wilson, "Tens of Thousands of Voters Drop Republican Affiliation after Capitol Riot," The Hill, January 27, 2021, thehill.com/homenews/state-watch/536113-tens-of-thou-sands-of-voters-drop-republican-affiliation-after-capitol.

146 "Desecrated our Capitol": Clare Hymes, Cassidy McDonald, and Eleanor Watson, "What We Know about the 'Unprecedented' U.S. Capitol Riot Arrests," CBS News, May 18, 2021, www.cbsnews.com/news/capitol-riot-arrests-2021-05-07/.

147 "Like long-serving Republican Pat Toomey": Emily Czachor, "Trump Retweets Claim GOP Senator Pat Toomey 'Complicit in' Massive Election Fraud," *Newsweek*, January 3, 2021, www.msn.com/en-us/news/politics/trump-retweets-claim-gop-senator-pat-toomey-complicit-in-massive-election-fraud/ar-BB1crf1I.

148 "Women are the single largest voting block": Samantha Schmidt, "The Gender Gap Was Expected to Be Historic. Instead, Women Voted Much as They Always Have," *Washington Post*, November 6, 2020, www.washingtonpost.com/dc-md-va/2020/11/06/election-2020-gender-gap-women/.

148 "Women broke for Biden": Erin Delmore, "This Is How Women Voters Decided the 2020 Election," NBC News, November 13, 2020, www.nbcnews.com/know-your-value/feature/how-women-voters-decided-2020-election-ncna1247746.

148 "More than 16 million Latinos voted": UCLA Latino Policy and Politics Initiative, "Latino Voters Were Decisive in 2020 Presidential Election," UCLA Newsroom, University of California

- Los Angeles, January 19, 2021, newsroom.ucla.edu/releases/
latino-vote-analysis-2020-presidential-election.

148 "More than half of Latinos": Thomas E. Patterson, "The Republicans'
Demographic Trap," *Boston Globe* (opinion), July 27, 2020, www.boston-
globe.com/2020/07/27/opinion/republicans-demographic-trap/.

149 "They have a great GOP profile": Thomas E. Patterson, "The
Republicans' Demographic Trap," *Boston Globe* (opinion),
July 27, 2020, www.bostonglobe.com/2020/07/27/opinion/
republicans-demographic-trap/.

149 "In 2020, however, they went Democratic": Kimmy
Yam, "Asian Americans Voted for Biden 63% to 31%, but
the Reality Is More Complex," NBC News, November
9, 2020, www.nbcnews.com/news/asian-america/
asian-americans-voted-biden-63-31-reality-more-complex-n1247171.

149 "It's worth noting white evangelicals": Thomas E. Patterson,
"The Republicans' Demographic Trap," *Boston Globe* (opinion),
July 27, 2020, www.bostonglobe.com/2020/07/27/opinion/
republicans-demographic-trap/.

149 "Independents went for Biden": "National Exit Polls: How Different
Groups Voted," *New York Times*, January 5, 2021, www.nytimes.com/
interactive/2020/11/03/us/elections/exit-polls-president.html.

149 "Only 32% of them view the GOP favorably": Jennifer
Harper, "GOP Image Takes a Hit, Says Gallup; Greatest Drop
among Republicans Themselves," *Washington Times*, February
10, 2021, www.washingtontimes.com/news/2021/feb/10/
gop-image-takes-a-hit-says-gallup-greatest-drop-am/.

150 "A full 50% of Independents": Eli Yokley, "Trump's Job Approval Hits
Unprecedented Low as Majority of Voters Say He Should Resign,"
Morning Consult, January 11, 2021, morningconsult.com/2021/01/11/
trump-approval-impeachment-resignation-polling/.

150 "In February 2021, for the first time": "Tracking Poll: Party Affiliation."
Gallup, March 27, 2021, news.gallup.com/poll/15370/Party-Affiliation.
aspx.

150 "We shouldn't miss that candidates": Yascha Mounk, "Lessons of the
2020 Election: What Democrats and Republicans Must Now Do to Win,"
Wall Street Journal, November 20, 2020, www.wsj.com/articles/lessons-
of-the-2020-election-what-democrats-and-republicans-must-now-do-
to-win-11605887801.

151 "The old trickle-down argument": Mara Liasson, "5 Lessons Democrats
Can Learn from the 2020 Elections," NPR.org, December 29, 2020,

www.npr.org/2020/12/29/949712778/5-lessons-democrats-can-learn-from-the-2020-elections.

151 "The number of Republican women": Danielle Kurtzleben, "How a Record Number of Republican Women Got Elected To Congress," NPR. org, November 13, 2020, www.npr.org/2020/11/13/934249216/how-a-record-number-of-republican-women-got-elected-to-congress; Jeffery Martin, "30th Republican Woman Could Join House as Judge Rules Claudia Tenney Winner in Disputed Race." *Newsweek*, February 6, 2021, www.msn.com/en-us/news/politics/30th-republican-woman-could-join-house-as-judge-rules-claudia-tenney-winner-in-disputed-race/ar-BB1dreFr.

151 "The party made inroads": Mara Liasson, "5 Lessons Democrats Can Learn From the 2020 Elections," NPR.org, December 29, 2020, www.npr.org/2020/12/29/949712778/5-lessons-democrats-can-learn-from-the-2020-elections.

151 "In fact, progressive champions": Yascha Mounk, "Lessons of the 2020 Election: What Democrats and Republicans Must Now Do to Win," *Wall Street Journal*, November 20, 2020, www.wsj.com/articles/lessons-of-the-2020-election-what-democrats-and-republicans-must-now-do-to-win-11605887801.

152 "He gained seven points among Asians": Kevin R. Kosar, "The Political Right Needs to Change Course on Elections Reform," American Enterprise Institute, February 1, 2021, www.aei.org/politics-and-public-opinion/the-political-right-needs-to-change-course-on-elections-reform/.

152 "That translated to him winning 61%": Andre Tartaret al., "Trump's New Latino Voters Are Sending Democrats a Message," Bloomberg.com, November 24, 2020, www.bloomberg.com/graphics/2020-us-election-hispanic-latino-voters/.

152 "In heavily Latino Southwest Texas": Yascha Mounk, "Lessons of the 2020 Election: What Democrats and Republicans Must Now Do to Win," *Wall Street Journal*, November 20, 2020, www.wsj.com/articles/lessons-of-the-2020-election-what-democrats-and-republicans-must-now-do-to-win-11605887801.

152 "In Zapata County": Brittany Bernstein, "The Latino Shift Toward Trump in South Texas: Anomaly or Realignment?" NationalReview. com, November 12, 2020, www.nationalreview.com/news/the-latino-shift-toward-trump-in-south-texas-anomaly-or-realignment/.

153 "The president earned 32%": Avik Roy, "No, Trump Didn't Win 'The Largest Share of Non-White Voters of Any Republican in 60

Years,'" *Forbes*, November 18, 2020, www.forbes.com/sites/theapothe-cary/2020/11/09/no-trump-didnt-win-the-largest-share-of-non-white-voters-of-any-republican-in-60-years/?sh=1267ab064a09.

155 "The third counting of Georgia ballots": Adrianne M. Haney, "Georgia Election Recount Results: Breaking down Final Numbers," 11Alive. com, WXIA Atlanta, December 7, 2020, www.11alive.com/article/news/politics/elections/georgia-election-recount-results-final-numbers/85-cbaacd70-f7e0-40ae-8dfa-3bf18f318645.

155 "If he'd gotten as many votes as our state's": William A. Galston, "Why Did House Democrats Underperform Compared to Joe Biden?" Brookings.edu, December 21, 2020, www.brookings.edu/blog/fixgov/2020/12/21/why-did-house-democrats-underperform-compared-to-joe-biden/.

158 "When the January 5 U.S. Senate runoff arrived": Buck Banks, "No-Shows, New Voters Swung Georgia Runoff Election," Pensito.com, February 3, 2021, www.pensito.com/2021/02/03/no-shows-new-voters-swung-georgia-runoff-election/.

158 "Our antics so motivated the opposition": Emma Hurt, "How Democrats Found Thousands of New Voters and Flipped Georgia's Senate Seats," NPR.org, February 6, 2021, www.npr.org/2021/02/06/964614820/how-democrats-found-thousands-of-new-voters-and-flipped-georgias-senate-seats.

159 "In January 2021, Gallup reported that 36%": Lydia Saad, "Americans' Political Ideology Held Steady in 2020," Gallup.com, January 11, 2021, news.gallup.com/poll/328367/americans-political-ideolo-gy-held-steady-2020.aspx.

159 "Across the country the GOP holds": "2021 Map: Republicans to Have Full Control of 23 States, Democrats 15," Americans for Tax Reform, November 9, 2020, www.atr.org/map?amp.

159 "We gained one more chamber": Kevin R. Kosar, "The Political Right Needs to Change Course on Elections Reform," American Enterprise Institute, February 1, 2021, www.aei.org/politics-and-public-opinion/the-political-right-needs-to-change-course-on-elections-reform/.

159 "In 22 states, voters gave Republicans control": Joe Walsh, "Republicans Will Enter 2021 with Control Over Most States' Governments. Here's Why That Matters for Redistricting," *Forbes*, November 6, 2020, www.forbes.com/sites/joewalsh/2020/11/06/republicans-will-enter-2021-with-control-over-most-states-governments-heres-why-that-matters-for-redistricting/?sh=6b21f23f441a.

159 "The 2020 election saw Republicans gain": Ally Mutnick and Anna

Gronewold, "GOP Wins Final 2020 House Race after Democrat
Concedes," Politico.com, February 9, 2021, www.msn.com/en-us/
news/politics/gop-wins-final-2020-house-race-after-democrat-concedes/
ar-BB1dvAss?ocid=uxbndlbing.

7: THE POWER OF MORE

191 "The Most Unbiased News Sources": Knight Foundation / Gallup,
"Perceived Accuracy and Bias in the News Media," KnightFoundation.
org, 2018, knightfoundation.org/wp-content/uploads/2020/03/
KnightFoundation_AccuracyandBias_Report_FINAL.pdf.

191 "The Most Biased News Sources": Knight Foundation / Gallup,
"Perceived Accuracy and Bias in the News Media," KnightFoundation.
org, 2018, knightfoundation.org/wp-content/uploads/2020/03/
KnightFoundation_AccuracyandBias_Report_FINAL.pdf.

8: THE 4CS: CHURCHES, CHARITIES, CORPORATIONS, CITIZENS

198 "Only three states have higher rates": Robert Fairlie and Sameeksha
Desai, "Early-Stage Entrepreneurship in the United States," Kauffman.
org, Ewing Marion Kauffman Foundation, 2020, indicators.kauffman.
org/wp-content/uploads/sites/2/2020/05/2019_Early-Stage-
Entrepreneurship-National-and-State-Report_final.pdf.

199 "The board's data-driven work": "Top Public Schools: National
Universities ," Usnews.com, U.S. News & World Report, 2021, www.
usnews.com/best-colleges/rankings/national-universities/top-public.

9: POLICY

214 "Republicans know small businesses": U.S. Small Business Administration:
Office of Advocacy, "2020 Small Business Profile," Advocacy.sba.gov, U.S.
Small Business Administration, 2021, cdn.advocacy.sba.gov/wp-content/
uploads/2020/06/04144224/2020-Small-Business-Economic-Profile-US.
pdf.

217 "During this past Republican administration's one term": "Budget and
Economic Data," Congressional Budget Office, 2021, www.cbo.gov/
about/products/budget-economic-data#2.

217 "2020 (not including C-19)": "The Budget and Economic Outlook:
2020 to 2030," Congressional Budget Office, January 28, 2020, www.
cbo.gov/publication/56020.

218 "At the end of 2020, 65%": Liz Hamel et al., "5 Charts About Public
Opinion on the Affordable Care Act and the Supreme Court," Kaiser
Family Foundation, December 18, 2020, www.kff.org/health-reform/

poll-finding/5-charts-about-public-opinion-on-the-affordable-care-act-
and-the-supreme-court/.

218 "And a full 45% of Republicans": "The New York Times / Siena College
National Poll," Siena College Research Institute, Siena College, October
20, 2020, scri.siena.edu/wp-content/uploads/2020/10/National-2-PR-
10-20-20-FINAL-1.pdf.

220 "One-in-ten Georgians": "Fact Sheet: Immigrants in Georgia,"
American Immigration Council, August 6, 2020, www.americanimmigra-
tioncouncil.org/research/immigrants-in-georgia.

220 "We also have an estimated 300,000+": "Profile of the Unauthorized
Population: Georgia," Migrationpolicy.org, Migration Policy
Institute, April 1, 2021, www.migrationpolicy.org/data/
unauthorized-immigrant-population/state/GA.

220 "We want them all to be safe": Hunter Hallman, "How Do
Undocumented Immigrants Pay Federal Taxes? An Explainer,"
Bipartisan Policy Center, March 28, 2018, bipartisanpolicy.org/blog/
how-do-undocumented-immigrants-pay-federal-taxes-an-explainer/.

223 "Less than half of non-whites support capital punishment": Jeffrey M.
Jones, "U.S. Support for Death Penalty Holds Above Majority Level,"
Gallup.com, November 19, 2020, news.gallup.com/poll/325568/
support-death-penalty-holds-above-majority-level.aspx.

224 "In 2020, voters re-elected 95%": Dave Beaudoin, "Ballotpedia's Daily
Brew: 94% of Incumbents Won Re-Election on Nov. 3—Here's the
Breakdown by State," Ballotpedia News, Lucy Burns Institute, January
27, 2021, news.ballotpedia.org/2021/01/27/ballotpedias-daily-brew-
94-of-incumbents-won-re-election-on-nov-3-heres-the-breakdown-by-
state/.

225 "Gallup's most recent polling": Joseph Lyttleton (ed. Brendan Monroe),
"The Debate over Congressional Term Limits, Explained," The
Millennial Source, February 3, 2021, themilsource.com/2021/01/29/
debate-over-congressional-term-limits-explained/.

225 "Likes a Florida State University study": Doug Bandow, "How to Term-
Limit Congress," *National Review*, January 29, 2019, www.nationalreview.
com/2019/01/congressional-term-limits-states/.

10: EMPATHY

236 "Just 40% of respondents": John Sides, "Surprisingly Few Voters
Think Trump Cares about 'People like Me,'" *Washington Post*,
March 26, 2020, www.washingtonpost.com/outlook/2020/03/26/
surprisingly-few-voters-think-trump-cares-about-people-like-me/.

237 "Under the Trump tax cuts": Shane Croucher, "Trump's 2017 Tax
    Cuts Helped Super-Rich Pay Lower Rate than Bottom 50 Percent:
    Economists," *Newsweek*, October 9, 2019, www.newsweek.com/
    trump-tax-cuts-jobs-act-wealth-economists-inequality-1464048.

238 "Still our party passed the bill": Hannah Lang, "Quinnipiac: Only 29%
    of Americans Approve of GOP Tax Plan," CNN.com, December 5, 2017,
    www.cnn.com/2017/12/05/politics/tax-plan-approval-quinnipiac-poll/
    index.html; Megan Brenan, "More Still Disapprove Than Approve of
    2017 Tax Cuts," Gallup.com, October 10, 2018, news.gallup.com/
    poll/243611/disapprove-approve-2017-tax-cuts.aspx.

238 "A year after the 2017 tax bill": Megan Brenan, "More Still Disapprove
    Than Approve of 2017 Tax Cuts," Gallup.com, October 10, 2018, news.
    gallup.com/poll/243611/disapprove-approve-2017-tax-cuts.aspx.

238 "The total national debt stood": "What Is the U.S. National Debt Right
    Now—and Why Is It So High?" Peter G. Peterson Foundation, accessed
    January 20, 2021, www.pgpf.org/national-debt-clock.

11: TONE

256 "Voters didn't trust the president": Salvador Rizzo and
    Glenn Kessler, "Trump's False or Misleading Claims
    Total 30,573 over 4 Years," *Washington Post*, February 10,
    2021, www.washingtonpost.com/politics/2021/01/24/
    trumps-false-or-misleading-claims-total-30573-over-four-years/.

257 "Their favorable opinion": Jack Brewster, "Poll: GOP's Popularity
    Plummets in Wake of Capitol Riot," *Forbes*, February 10, 2021, www.
    forbes.com/sites/jackbrewster/2021/02/10/poll-gops-popularity-plum-
    mets-in-wake-of-capitol-riot/?sh=17060b0e583a.

258 "The *Wall Street Journal* and *Fox News* register": Knight Foundation
    / Gallup Survey, "Perceived Accuracy and Bias in the News Media,"
    KnightFoundation.org, 2018, knightfoundation.org/wp-content/
    uploads/2020/03/KnightFoundation_AccuracyandBias_Report_FINAL.
    pdf.

258 "In Fall 2020, 89% of Republicans": Megan Brenan, "Americans Remain
    Distrustful of Mass Media," Gallup.com, September 30, 2020, news.
    gallup.com/poll/321116/americans-remain-distrustful-mass-media.aspx.

261 "Newsmax quickly posted a telling disclaimer": Newsmax Wires,
    "Facts About Dominion, Smartmatic You Should Know," Newsmax.
    com, December 19, 2020, www.newsmax.com/us/smartmat-
    ic-dominion-voting-systems-software-election/2020/12/19/
    id/1002355/.

261 "Consequently, at the end of January 2021": Nick Laughlin and Peyton Shelburne, "How Voters' Trust in Elections Shifted in Response to Biden's Victory," Morning Consult, January 27, 2021, morningconsult. com/form/tracking-voter-trust-in-elections/.

261 "At the same time, 98% of Democrats": Daniel A. Cox, "After the Ballots Are Counted: Conspiracies, Political Violence, and American Exceptionalism," The Survey Center on American Life, February 11, 2021, www.americansurveycenter.org/research/after-the-bal-lots-are-counted-conspiracies-political-violence-and-american-exception-alism/.

261 "Made 53% of Democrats more motivated": Nick Laughlin and Peyton Shelburne, "How Voters' Trust in Elections Shifted in Response to Biden's Victory," Morning Consult, January 27, 2021, morningconsult. com/form/tracking-voter-trust-in-elections/.

261 "They think using violence": Tom Gjelten, "A 'Scary' Survey Finding: 4 In 10 Republicans Say Political Violence May Be Necessary," NPR.org, February 11, 2021, www.npr.org/2021/02/11/966498544/a-scary-sur-vey-finding-4-in-10-republicans-say-political-violence-may-be-necessa.

261 "Nearly 30% of Republicans believe false": Daniel A. Cox, "After the Ballots Are Counted: Conspiracies, Political Violence, and American Exceptionalism," The Survey Center on American Life, February 11, 2021, www.americansurveycenter.org/research/after-the-bal-lots-are-counted-conspiracies-political-violence-and-american-exception-alism/.

261 "One last fruit of misinformation": Aaron Blake, "The Most Important Thing Donald Trump Said in His CPAC Speech," *Washington Post*, February 28, 2021, www.msn.com/en-us/news/politics/the-most-important-thing-donald-trump-said-in-his-cpac-speech/ar-BB1e68yU?ocid=uxbndlbing.